THE FALLEN MAN
AGAIN CAN SOAR

BUT WOMAN FALLS
TO RISE NO MORE

Barroom Ballads

Convivially Collected by
FRANK SHAY
Magnificently Illuminated by
JOHN HELD JR.

Dover Publications, Inc., New York

Published in Canada by General Publishing Company, Ltd., 30 Lesmill Road, Don Mills, Toronto, Ontario.

Published in the United Kingdom by Constable and Company, Ltd., 10 Orange Street, London WC 2.

This Dover edition, first published in 1961, under the title *My Pious Friends and Drunken Companions and More Pious Friends and Drunken Companions* is an unabridged republication of the text of the following works:

My Pious Friends and Drunken Companions as originally published by The Macaulay Company in 1927.

More Pious Friends and Drunken Companions as originally published by The Macaulay Company in 1928.

The illustrations for this edition have been selected from among those in the first editions. This edition was designed by Bernard Etter.

International Standard Book Number: 0-486-20946-6
Library of Congress Catalog Card Number: 61-66216

Manufactured in the United States of America
Dover Publications, Inc.
180 Varick Street
New York, N. Y. 10014

Contents

MY PIOUS FRIENDS AND DRUNKEN COMPANIONS

Over the Burning Sands—Introduction *xi*
Abdullah Bul-Bul Amir *3*
The Band Played On *6*
O! Susanna *8*
Sam Bass *9*
Brother Noah *10*
The Butcher's Boy *12*
Casey Jones *13*
Casey Jones II *15*
Navy Fragment *16*
Forty-nine Bottles *17*
Ach, Du Lieber Augustine *17*
I Wanta Go Home *17*
In the Sweet Bye and Bye *17*
Christofo Columbo *18*
Clementine *23*
When I Die *24*
One More Drink for the Four of Us *25*
Sweet Rosie *25*
The Foggy, Foggy Dew *26*
A Catch *26*
The Ballad of Captain Kidd *27*
The Old Grey Mare *29*
The Dying Hobo *30*
Way Down Yonder in the Cornfield *31*
The Lamentable History of Frankie and Johnnie *31*
Just a Wee Doch-an-Dorris *36*
Hail, Hail! *36*

The Dying Fisherman's Song 37
I Had But Fifty Cents 38
I've Been Workin' on the Railroad 39
Little Brown Jug 40
I Know Where They Are 41
I'm Full 41
Jesse James 42
Back and Side Go Bare, Go Bare! 43
Fill the Flowing Bowl 45
Le Chef de Gare 46
The Ballad of Lydia Pinkham 46
Railroad Bill 48
The Morning After 50
The Oregon Trail 51
O'Slattery's Light Dragoons 52
Samuel Hall 54
Down Among the Dead Men 55
It's the Sime the 'Ole World Over 56
It's the Sime the 'Ole World Over II 58
That Tattooed French Lady 59
The Son of a Gambolier 59
Water Boy 61
There Is a Tavern in the Town 62
Wal, I Swan 64
Young Charlotte 66
Whiskey for My Johnny 70
I Wish I Was Single Again 71
Rolling Home 72
Oh! Oh! Oh! It's a Lovely War! 74
Maid of Amsterdam 76
Mademoiselle from Armentieres 78
The Cowboy's Lament 80
The Face on the Bar-room Floor 82
Twenty Years Ago 84
Lasca 86
'Ostler Joe 90

The Kid's Fight 96
Don't Go in them Lions' Cage Tonight, Mother 100
The High Barbaree 102
The Marines' Song 105

MORE PIOUS FRIENDS AND DRUNKEN COMPANIONS

Here's to Crime—Introduction 111
A Pack of Cards. 117
The Roving Gambler 120
Australian Highwayman's Song 122
Our Gude-Man 124
Down in Dear Old Greenwich Village 128
The Wreck of the Old 97 131
The Female Smuggler 132
O, Give Me a Home Where the Buffalo Roam 134
Heenan and Sayers 136
Rio Grande 138
False Henry 139
The Charming Young Widow I Met on the Train 140
Hop Head 143
Salvation Army Song 144
Hannah 145
The Cannibal Maiden 146
Life Is But a Game of Cards 147
Pictures from Life's Other Side 148
Old Joe Clark 149
Cocaine Bill and Morphine Sue 150
Rollicking Bill the Sailor 151
Texas Rangers 152
Cocaine Lil and Morphine Sue 153
Oh, No, John! 154
Duckfoot Sue 155
Willie the Weeper 156
Hop Song 157
Johnny Sands 158

A Little More Cider *160*
Lucky Jim *161*
The Boston Burglar *162*
Fair Fanny Moore *164*
I've Only Been Down to the Club *165*
Springfield Mountain *166*
My Cottage by the Sea *167*
The Hell-bound Train *168*
Drunkard John *170*
Once I Loved a Railroad Brakeman *173*
Ballad of a Young Man *174*
The Dog-Catcher's Child *176*
Je Donnerais Versailles *177*
The Sailor's Return *178*
The Caissons Are Rolling Along *179*
Young Monroe at Gerry's Rock *180*
The Midnight Express *182*
Bible Stories *184*
When You and I Were Young, Maggie *188*
Seven Long Years *190*
The Letter Edged in Black *192*
I'll Give My Love a Cherry *194*
Jim Fisk, Jr. *195*
What's the Use? *198*
Get Away, Old Man, Get Away! *199*
Dis Mornin', Dis Evenin', So Soon *200*
The Dying Ranger *202*
Shanahan's Ould Shebeen *205*
Sally Brown *207*
The Recruit *208*
The Flying Cloud *210*
The Girl in the Blue Velvet Band *213*
The Millman Tragedy *217*
In Bohemia Hall *220*
The Actor's Story *222*

Index of Song Titles *227*
Index of First Lines and Choruses *231*

My Pious Friends and Drunken Companions

Songs and Ballads of Conviviality
Collected by FRANK SHAY

Magnificently Illuminated *by* JOHN HELD JR.

"Pure water is the best of
 gifts that man to man can bring.
But who am I that I should have
 the best of anything?
Let princes revel at the pump,
 let peers with ponds make free,
Whiskey or wine, or even beer,
 is good enough for me."

Neaves.

Over the Burning Sands

All Americans are two or three drinks below normal. This simple statement will not be at all startling to the ballad-lover. He is only too well aware that without the immediate aid of alcoholic stimulant our landsmen cannot be induced to loose their tongues in song. A lethargic and inhibited crew, my merry fellows. Only with such assistance are we able to get the lead out of our feet and the frogs from our throats: not until we are pleasantly whiffled are we able to break down those walls of puritanic repression that seem to be our only birthright. Now that we are deprived of our tipple it is highly probable we will lapse into a dolorous and lugubrious silence unbroken save by a highly moralistic interference.

There was a period not so long gone, a time contemptuously called Victorian but which is now receiving the favourable attention of our most advanced historians, when we rose to the heights. It was our nearest approach to urbanity, a time when we sang and drank and danced, though we did all three quite badly. Given an even break we might have sloughed off our amateurishness and become a truly festive nation. Like all drinkers we were good fellows when we had it. . . .

Can you recall those days? The Naughty Nineties? The days when the words "naughty" and "wicked" were still uncorrupted; when a professed preference for the company of widows marked you a man of the world, a gay man-about-town? When the places that dispensed liquid refreshment had swinging doors and were called saloons: when the very best cost but fifteen cents; when a bender was called a bun; when a man who was frequently intoxicated was an old toper and not a souse? Those were the days! The never-to-be-forgotten Nineties, the dear, dead days that are gone forever.

Those were the days! Our first impulse when pleasantly jingled was to burst into mellifluous song. It required but a few similarly stimulated males to make a party. In those dear days girls were parlor fixtures and did not intrude upon the provinces of men. Far be it from the purpose of this indifferent commentator to deplore today's customs: in many ways we have a better time for their presence, a much better time indeed.

Let's get back to our party at the bar. The impulse to sing came quite early in the proceedings. Joe, he of the nervous fingers, would suggest the party retire to the back room and see if the piano was working. It was a very obvious stall: each of you knew why you went towards the piano but you continued to talk of other matters. You talked largely of Congress and the situation in Cuba, you were outspoken in your condemnation of Spain and you strongly advised American interference. More homely matters such as Irish Maggie's new baby and how the least Tim could do was to marry the girl; it was what was expected of a gentleman. Perhaps Joe didn't care much for the opinions being aired and hummed a few bars of "There'll Be a Hot Time In the Old Town Tonight" or "After the Ball." Down deep in your innocent hearts you knew this was all preparatory to the real business at hand. Joe was at the piano. Even before the sweet singer of the old Ninth Ward got on his favorites the group essayed a close harmony number, quite likely "Way Down Yonder In the Cornfield." You probably found room for complaint; the tenor was off, the second couldn't lead or something was sour. There was nothing to do but to order another round. You sat over your drink awaiting the great moment. Then Jim, who was married, got up and said he'd have to be going along before it got too late: Bill recalled that he had promised his wife he'd get up early the next morning and mow the lawn before he went to work.

Joe and Tom, bachelors, seeing their nice little party going to the dogs resolved upon stern measures. Joe turned again to the piano and picked out "I Wish I Was Single Again" in a provoking manner to make the two married men tarry a bit longer. Didn't the single fellows have all the fun? Jim and Bill would stay for just one more round if Joe would sing "Clementine." Joe did and added "Young Charlotte" for good measure. Thus heartened Joe opened the floodgates of song. He added, with the usual concomitant of beverage, "The High Barbaree" and "There is a Tavern in the Town." "Abdullah Bul-Bul Amir" was a long song and could only be appreciated by an encore round. They tried, collectively of course, "Frankie and Johnnie" and "Christofo Columbo," punctuated by more libations and met "Casey Jones" like an old friend. "The Cowboy's Lament" and "Lydia Pinkham" came, spent a few minutes, and were toasted out of the party. On and on they went through their repertory truly happy and almost free. They could not know that within a few short years their whiskey tenors and booze baritones were to be stilled forever.

The evening wore on. New members attached themselves to the party and some dropped out. Just about the time they were resinging some numbers the barkeep came in and apologetically asked the boys to have one on the house, a night cap, the place was closing and he was only obeying the law. Funny thing, in those wet and depraved days we had an inordinate respect for the law that today is quite lacking. A hurried round to polish off the night, a little close harmony on "I've Been Working On the Railroad" and out into the stilly night. Perhaps we were a little wobbly on our feet; the cop on the beat winked an eye and turned his head the other way. A good night's sleep, a bath in the morning and we were none the worse for our festal night.

The songs in this little volume are in a manner snatched from that era and those jongleurs. The music-lover who frequents the symphony concerts and delves deep into the works of Wagner and Debussy will dismiss them as trivial. He will point, if you persist, to their clichés, to their assonances and to their lack of true melody. If you attempt to sing them he will cover his ears with his hands and appeal to some ceiling deity to protect him from their dissonances. The folk-lorist will dismiss them with the phrases profane and vulgar. To him they are but the product of low resorts, gutter songs, the communal musical expression of an artistically destitute society.

My title needs a word of explanation. Away back in the good old days of long ago I found myself eagerly seeking a homestead in what was happily called "the last great West." At Tête Jaune Cache there was a straw boss known locally as "Blackie." The cockneys referred to him as "a bit of a breed" and perhaps he was. Maybe he had a bit of black or red blood mixed in with the white. He commanded our respect in a very unbreedlike way and held it as such is held out where men were supposed to be men. Blackie would get rousingly drunk, not at the Pass but in Edmonton, hammer on the bar and demand further drinks for his pious friends and drunken companions, one of which, happily at those times, I happened to be.

In using Blackie's kriegspiel I have rendered tribute where it is due and I have successfully included the two vastly different audiences for drinking songs: the singing hydropot and the warbling guzzler.

The former puts a great deal more feeling into songs glorifying inebriation than the authors ever hoped for, and the latter sings those songs in which there is little or no mention of drink or drinking. The white-ribbon lads lift their thin voices trying hard to animate the words of Ben Jonson's "Drink To Me Only With Thine Eyes" fully convinced they are singing a devilish, ribald song straight from hell's gaudy gin-mills. Any half-hearted soak could tell them it is no more a drinking song than Stevenson's "Sixteen Men on a Dead Man's Chest" is a pirate's song.

The so-called drinking songs, the songs that glorify the drinking of spiritous and fermented liquors, are weak and vapid things at their best. Almost without exception they carry the smell of the oil-lighted library lamp and show the literary striving for rhyme and effect. Only on occasion do they rise to such glory as: "The rolling English drunkard made the rolling English road" and only Chesterton could achieve that. The modern minne-singers, Belloc, Masefield and Maynard sing, for the most part, of beer and skittles and sometimes they attempt to celebrate the virtues of the lowly cider. The honest and simple reveler much prefers the sentimental and melancholy ballads.

These then are the songs professional drinkers sing when in a convivial mood. They are presented in all their tawdry garments, unprettified save that in some cases their faces and hands have been washed so they may properly appear in company. Their assonances, defective rhythms, their atrocious rhetoric, their vulgarities have been retained. As far as possible they go to you as they were sung in their prime with the hope that in your enforced aridity they may still give some pleasure.

Some were first heard in the haunts of Blackie; others came from a little Spanish bosun on a Standard Oil tankship and some from two members of the crew of the same ship, some from the sea-coast gin-mills frequented by sailors, some from the army camps in this country and France. Not a few were first heard in Luke O'Connor's Working Girl's Home, where Masefield found honorable employment serving the suds to old Ninth Warders, others in The Golden Swan, known to the literate and *cognoscenti* as The Hell Hole, still others came from homes, studios and clubs. Wherever it has been possible I have given the singer credit on the page with the ballad: a tricky memory may have slighted many, I can only ask their indulgence and acknowledge their help and interest in this manner.

Readers, meet my pious friends and drunken companions: I think you ought to know and like each other.

FRANK SHAY

Provincetown, Mass.
May 1, 1927

Acknowledgments

It is more with pleasure and honor than from any sense of duty that I acknowledge the expert and valuable assistance given me in compiling this work by Miss Helen Ramsey and Mr. Robert A. Slavin. Mine alone was the pleasurable task to listen and decide the contents: theirs to set down the words and shoehorn them into the melodies. Thanks, too, are due to Miss Packey Leveson and Miss Judith Tobey, to Messrs. James E. Harris, Adolf Bergman, William H. Wells, Cardwell Thompson, John Held, Jr., George Cronyn, Clinton Jonas, H. Douglas Hadden, Charles Somerville, and others who must remain anonymous.

"The Cowboy's Lament" is used by courtesy of John A. Lomax and the Macmillan Company.

Mr. Held's felicitous woodcuts are used through the courtesy of *The New Yorker* and editors of *Vanity Fair* and the Weyhe Gallery.

F. S.

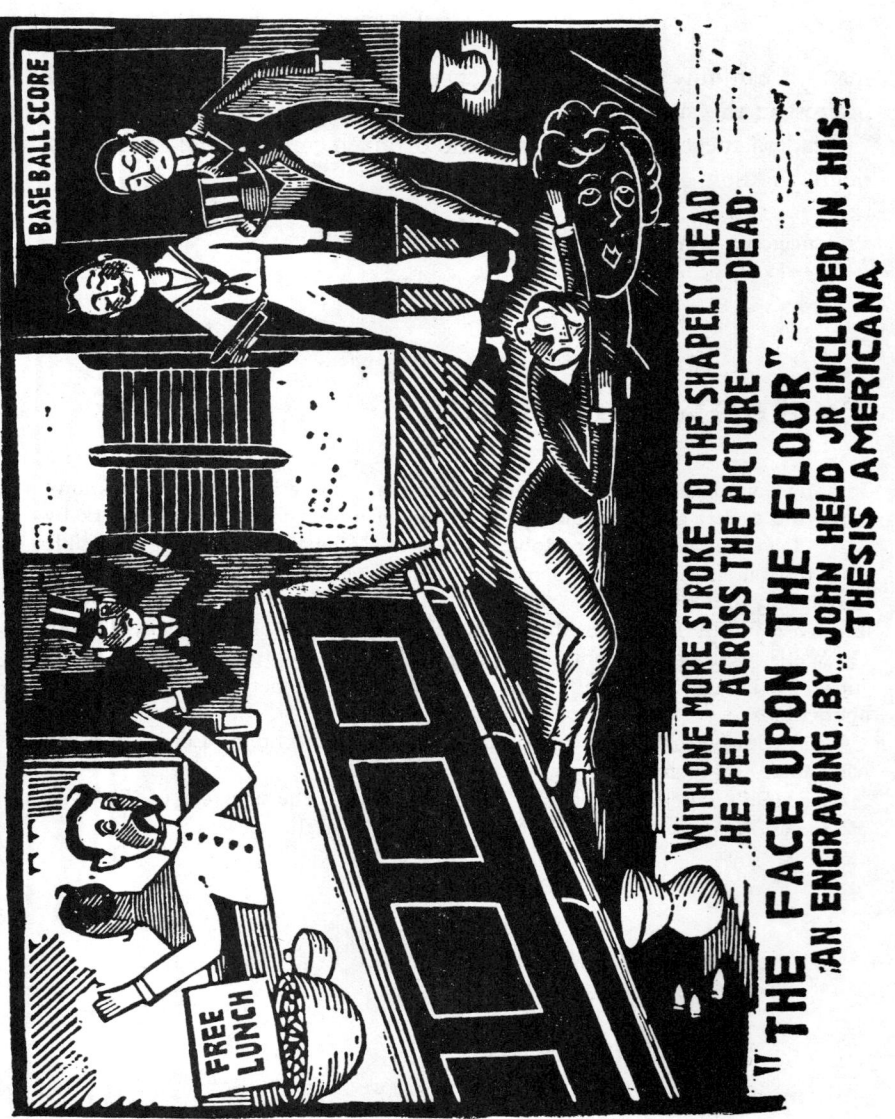

My Pious Friends and Drunken Companions

Abdullah Bul-Bul Amir*

When they needed a man to encourage the van
   Or harass the foe from the rear,
Or storm a redoubt, they had only to shout
   For Abdullah Bul-Bul Amir.

There are men of renown and well known to fame
   In the army that's led by the czar,
But the best known of all was a man by the name
   Of Ivan Petrovsky Skivar.

  *Sometimes known as Abdul A-Bul-Bul Amir.

He could imitate Irving, play poker and pool,
  And strum on the Spanish guitar;
In fact quite the cream of the Muscovite team,
  Was Ivan Petrovsky Skivar.

One day this bold Russian he shouldered his gun
  And with his most truculent sneer,
Was looking for fun when he happened to run
  Upon Abdullah Bul-Bul Amir.

"Young man," said Bul-Bul, "is existence so dull
  That you're anxious to end your career?
For infidel know you have trod on the toe
  Of Abdullah Bul-Bul Amir."

Said Ivan, "My friend, your remarks in the end
  Will avail you but little, I fear,
For you never will survive to repeat them alive,
  Mr. Abdullah Bul-Bul Amir."

"O, take one last look at this cool shady nook,
  And send your regrets to the czar.
By which I imply you are going to die,
  Mr. Ivan Petrovsky Skivar."

Then this haughty Mameluke drew his trusty skibouk,
  And shouting "Allah Akbar,"
And on murder bent he ferociously went
  For Ivan Petrovsky Skivar.

As Abdullah's long knife was extracting the life,
  In fact, as he shouted "Huzzah,"
He felt himself struck by that wily Kalmuck,
  Count Ivan Petrovsky Skivar.

The Sultan rode up the disturbance to quell,
  Expecting the victor to cheer,
But he only drew nigh to hear the last sigh,
  Of Abdullah Bul-Bul Amir.

Czar Petrovich too, in his uniform blue,
  Rode up in his new crested car,
He arrived just in time to exchange a last line
  With Ivan Petrovsky Skivar.

On a stone by the banks where the Danube doth roll,
  Engraved in characters clear,
Is "Stranger, remember to pray for the soul,
  Of Abdullah Bul-Bul Amir."

A Muscovite maid her long vigil doth keep,
  Alone 'neath the cold northern star,
And the name that she murmurs in vain as she weeps,
  Is Ivan Petrovsky Skivar.

The Band Played On

1. Matt Casey formed a social club that beat the town for style,
    And hired for a meeting place a hall;
    When pay day came around each week they greased the floor with wax,
    And danced with noise and vigor at the ball.
    Each Saturday you'd see them dressed up in Sunday clothes,
    Each lad would have his sweetheart by his side.
    When Casey led the first grand march they all would fall in line,
    Behind the man who was their joy and pride.
        For—

Chorus :

Casey would waltz with a strawberry blonde,
    And the band played on,
He'd glide 'cross the floor with the girl he ador'd.
    And the band played on,
But his brain was so loaded it nearly exploded,
The poor girl would shake with alarm.
He'd never leave the girl with the strawberry curl,
    And the band played on.

2. Such kissing in the corner and such whispering in the hall,
    And telling tales of love behind the stairs—
    As Casey was the favorite and he that ran the ball,
    Of kissing and love-making did his share.
    At twelve o'clock exactly they all would fall in line,
    Then march down to the dining-hall and eat.
    But Casey would not join them although every thing was fine,
    But he stayed upstairs and exercised his feet.
        For—

Chorus

3. Now when the dance was over and the band played "Home Sweet Home,"
   They played a tune at Casey's own request.
He thanked them very kindly for the favors they had shown,
   Then he'd waltz once with the girl he loved best.
Most all the friends are married that Casey used to know,
   And Casey too has taken him a wife.
The blonde he used to waltz and glide with on the ballroom floor,
   Is happy Missis Casey now for life.
      For—

Chorus

O! Susanna

I came from Alabama
    Wid my banjo on my knee;
I'm gwine to Louisiana,
    My true love for to see.
It rained all night the day I left,
    The weather it was dry,
The sun so hot I froze to death;
    Susanna, don't you cry.

Chorus :

O! Susanna, O don't you cry for me;
    I've come from Alabama
Wid my banjo on my knee.

I jumped aboard de telegraph
    And trabbled down the ribber,
De 'lectric fluid magnified
    And killed five hundred nigger;
De bullgine bust, de horse run off,
    I really thought I'd die;
I shut my eyes, to hold my breath;
    Susanna, don't you cry.

Chorus

I had a dream de odder night
    When ebery t'ing was still;
I thought I saw Susanna
    A-coming down the hill;
The buckwheat cake was in her mouth,
    The tear was in her eye;
Says I, "I'm coming from the South,
    Susanna, don't you cry."

Chorus

I soon will be in New Orleans,
   And den I'll look all round,
And when I find Susanna
   I will fall upon the ground;
And if I do not find her
   Dis darkie'll surely die,
And when I'm dead and buried,
   Susanna, don't you cry.

Chorus

Sam Bass

Sam Bass was born in Indiana, it was his native home,
   And at the age of seventeen young Sam began to roam.
Sam first came out to Texas a cowboy for to be;
   A kinder-hearted fellow you seldom ever see.

Now Sam left the Collins ranch in the merry month of May,
   With a herd of Texas cattle the Black Hills for to see.
Sold out in Custer City, went on an awful spree;
   A tougher lot of cowboys the country never see.

In coming back from Denver they robbed the U. P. train,
   They then split up in parties and started out again.
Joe Collins and his partners were overtaken soon,
   And with all their hard-earned money they had to meet their doom.

Sam made it back to Texas, all right side up with care,
   Rode into the town of Denton with all his friends to share.
But his career was short in Texas, three robberies did he do,
   He held up all the passengers, the mail and express cars, too.

Sam had four companions, four brave and daring lads:
   They were Richardson, Jackson, Joe Collins and Old Dad;
Four more bold and daring cowboys the ranchers never knew,
   They whipped the Texas Rangers and ran the boys in blue.

10 Brother Noah

Sam had another companion, called Arkansaw for short,
   He was shot by a Texas Ranger by the name of Thomas Fort.
O, Tom was a big six-footer and thought him mighty fly,
   But I can tell you his racket, he was a deadbeat on the sly.

Jim Murphy borrowed Sam's good gold and then refused to pay,
   The only shot he fired was to give poor Sam away.
Jim sold out Sam and Barnes and left their friends to mourn,
   But what a scorching Jim will get when Gabriel blows his horn.

Sam Bass met his fate at Round Rock, July the twenty-first,
   They filled poor Sam with rifle balls and emptied out his purse,
And now he is a corpse and his body turned to clay,
   And Jackson's gone to Mexico and there I guess he'll stay.

Brother Noah

2. No, you can't sir, no, you can't, sir,
    You can't come into the ark of the Lord
   Though it's growing very dark and it's raining very hard.
    Halleloo, halleloo, halleloo, hallelujah!

3. Very well, sir, very well, sir,
    You can go to the dickens with your darned old scow,
   'Cause it ain't goin' to rain very hard no how.
    Halleloo, halleloo, halleloo, hallelujah!

4. That's a lie, sir, that's a lie, sir,
    You can darn soon tell that it ain't no sell,
   'Cause it's sprinklin' now and it's goin' to rain like hell.
    Halleloo, halleloo, halleloo, hallelujah!

The Butcher's Boy

2. There is a house in this same town,
   Where my true love goes and sits him down;
   He takes a strange girl on his knee,
   And tells her what he won't tell me.

3. 'Tis grief for me, I'll tell you why,
   Because she has more gold than I;
   Her gold will melt and silver fly,
   She'll see the day she's poor as I.

4. I went upstairs to make my bed,
   And nothing to my mother said,
   I took a chair and sit me down,
   With pen and ink I wrote it down.

*Some versions have it "Dublin City": Boston City, in fact, New York City, will serve equally well. Obviously it is the natural brother of "There Is a Tavern In The Town."

5. On every line I dropped a tear,
   While calling home my Willie dear. . . .
   Her father he came home that night,
   "Where, Oh where has my darling gone?"

6. He went upstairs, the door he broke,
   And found her hanging by a rope.
   He took his knife and cut her down,
   And on her breast these lines he found:

7. "Go dig my grave both wide and deep,
   Place a marble stone at my head and feet.
   Upon my breast a marble dove
   To show them that I died for love."

Casey Jones*

Come all you rounders if you want to hear,
A story about a brave engineer,
Casey Jones was the rounder's name,
On a six-eight wheeler, boys, he won his fame.
The caller called Casey at half past four,
Kissed his wife at the station door,
Mounted to the cabin with his orders in his hand,
And took his farewell trip to that promised land.

   Casey Jones! Mounted to the cabin,
   Casey Jones with his orders in his hand.
   Casey Jones! Mounted to his cabin,
   And took his farewell trip to that promised land.

Put in your water and shovel in your coal,
Put your head out the window, watch them drivers roll,
I'll run her till she leaves the rail,
'Cause I'm eight hours late with that western mail.

*Literally K. C. Jones; Kansas City Jones.
Copyright 1909. Copyright Renewed 1936 and Assigned to Shapiro, Bernstein & Co., New York. Used by permission.

14 Casey Jones

He looked at his watch, and his watch was slow,
He looked at his water and the water was low,
He turned to the fireman and he said,
"We're going to reach Frisco but we'll all be dead."

    Casey Jones! Going to reach Frisco,
    Casey Jones! But we'll all be dead.
    Casey Jones! Going to reach Frisco,
    We're going to reach Frisco, but we'll all be dead.

Casey pulled up that Reno hill,
He tooted for the crossing with an awful shrill,
The switchman knew by the engine's moans
That the man at the throttle was Casey Jones.
He pulled up within two miles of the place,
Number Four stared him right in the face,
Turned to the fireman, said, "Boy, you'd better jump,
'Cause there's two locomotives that's a-going to bump."

    Casey Jones! Two locomotives!
    Casey Jones! That's a-going to bump!
    Casey Jones! Two locomotives!
    There's two locomotives that's a-going to bump.

Casey said just before he died,
"There's two more roads that I'd like to ride."
Fireman said, "What could they be?"
"The Southern Pacific and the Santa Fe."
Mrs. Jones sat on her bed a-sighing,
Just received a message that Casey was dying,
Said, "Go to bed, children, and hush your crying,
'Cause you got another papa on the Salt Lake Line."

    Casey Jones! Got another papa!
    Casey Jones! On that Salt Lake Line!
    Casey Jones! Got another papa!
    And you've got another papa on that Salt Lake Line.

Casey Jones II

A more artless variant was heard on a Canadian Northern work train out where, as the travel brochures have it, the "last great West begins":

Come all you rounders for I want you to hear
The story told of a brave engineer;
Casey Jones was the rounder's name
On a heavy six-eight wheeler he rode to fame.

Caller called Jones about half past four,
Jones kissed his wife at the station door,
Climbed into the cab with the orders in his hand,
Says, "This is my trip to the promised land."

Through South Memphis yards on the fly,
He heard the firemen say, "You've got a white-eye."
All the switchmen knew by the engine's moans,
That the hogger at the throttle was Casey Jones.

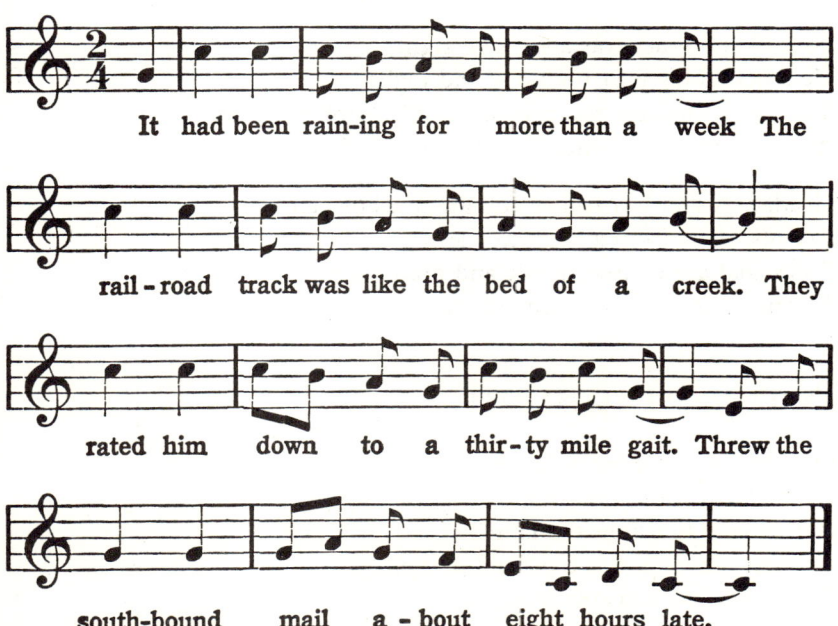

It had been rain-ing for more than a week The rail-road track was like the bed of a creek. They rated him down to a thir-ty mile gait. Threw the south-bound mail a-bout eight hours late.

*Music Copyright 1909. Copyright Renewed 1936 and Assigned to Shapiro, Bernstein & Co., Inc., New York. Used by permission.

Fireman says, "Casey, you're runnin' too fast,
You run the block signal the last station you passed."
Jones says, "Yes, I think we can make it, though,
For she steams much better than ever I know."

Jones says, "Fireman, don't you fret,
Keep knockin' at the firedoor, don't give up yet;
I'm goin' to run her till she leaves the rail
Or make it on time with the south-bound mail."

Around the curve and a-down the dump,
Two locomotives were a-bound to bump,
Fireman hollered, "Jones, it's just ahead,
We might jump and make it but we'll all be dead."

'Twas around this curve he saw a passenger train,
Something happened in Casey's brain;
Fireman jumped off, but Jones stayed on,
He's a good engineer but he's dead and gone.

Poor Casey Jones was always all right,
He stuck to his post both day and night:
They loved to hear the whistle of old Number Three
As he came into Memphis on the old K. C.

Headaches and heartaches and all kinds of pain
Are not apart from a railroad train;
Tales that are earnest, noble and gran'
Belong to the life of a railroad man.

Navy Fragment

Oh, the captain went below,
For to light the cabin lamp;
But he couldn't light the lamp
Because the wick was too dam' damp.
Heave-ho, you sons of glory,
   The Golden Gates are passed.

Forty-nine Bottles

Forty-nine bottles hanging on the wall.
Forty-nine bottles hanging on the wall.
Take one away from them all,
Forty-eight bottles hanging on the wall.
Continue ad lib, ad nauseam.

Ach, Du Lieber Augustine

Ach du lieber Augustine, Augustine, Augustine,
Ach du lieber Augustine alles ist hin!
Geld ist weg, Mädl ist weg, alles weg, alles weg,
Ach du lieber Augustine alles ist hin!

I Wanta Go Home

I wanta go home, I wanta go home,
The bullets they whistle, the cannons they roar.
I don't wanta go to the trenches no more.
Ship me over the sea,
Where the Allemand can't get at me:
O, my! I'm too young to die,
I wanta go home!

In the Sweet Bye and Bye

Long haired preachers come out every night,
   Try to tell you what's wrong and what's right;
But when asked about something to eat,
   They will answer in accents so sweet:

     You will eat bye and bye,
     In the glorious land of the sky.
       Work and pray,
       Live on hay,
     You'll have pie in the sky when you die!

Christofo Columbo

2. Columbus came from Italee,
    He was full of pink confetti
　He showed the Queen of Spain,
    How to manage her spaghetti.

> Oh, Christofo Columbo,
> Knew land it could be found-o,
> That heathen-hating, navigating,
> Son-of-a-gun, Columbo!

3. He rushed up to the Queen one day,
    Said, "Give me ships and cargo,
　I'll be a sea-going, son-of-a-gun
    If I don't bring back Chicago."

> Oh, Christofo Columbo,
> He thought the world was round-o,
> That encroaching, queen-approaching,
> Son-of-a-gun, Columbo!

4. The Queen she said to Ferdinand,
    "His scheme sounds like a daisy."
　"To hell with him," said Ferdinand,
    "I think the wop is crazy."

> Oh, Christofo Columbo,
> He thought the world was round-o,
> That pioneering, buccaneering,
> Son-of-a-gun, Columbo!

5. "It isn't ships or men he wants,
    For something else he's shootin',
　And if he hangs around you much,
    He'll lose his head right tootin'.

> Oh, Christofo Columbo,
> Knew that gold could be found-o,
> That brave seafaring, never-caring,
> Son-of-a-gun, Columbo!

6. Said Columbo, "Now, Isabelle,
    Don't act so gosh darned funny,
  I need the ships and the men
    So pony up the money."

   Oh, Christofo Columbo,
   He knew ships could be found-o,
   That always busted, never trusted,
   Son-of-a-gun, Columbo!

7. Said Isabelle, "Now wait awhile,
    And cut out this flam-flimmin';
  You've only asked for ships and men
    But how about some wimmin?"

   Oh, Christofo Columbo,
   He knew the world was round-o,
   This goll-durning, woman spurning
   Son-of-a-gun, Columbo!

8. On the day they sailed away,
    The people thought them crazy.
  Columbus said, "No janes on board,
    The sailors won't get lazy."

   Oh, Christofo Columbo,
   Never could be bound-o,
   That woman-hating, captivating
   Son-of-a-gun, Columbo!

9. In fourteen hundred and ninety-two,
    Across the broad Atlantic;
  The sailors all were filled with grief,
    Their wives were nearly frantic.

   Oh, Christofo Columbo,
   He knew the world was round-o,
   That family-breaking, history-making,
   Son-of-a-gun, Columbo!

10. In fourteen hundred and ninety-two,
     The doctors were not many,
  The only one they had on board
     Was a gosh-darned quack named Benny.

         Oh, Christofo Columbo,
         He knew the world was round-o,
         That philosophic, philanthropic,
         Son-of-a-gun, Columbo!

11. Colombo's ears ached him one day,
     But Benny was quite placid.
  He filled up both Columbo's ears,
     With hot mercuric acid.

         Oh, Christofo Columbo,
         Knew doctors could be drowned-o,
         That democratic and autocratic,
         Son-of-a-gun, Columbo!

12. They anchored near San Salvydor,
     In search of women and booty;
  A pretty girl stood on the shore,
     Columbo said, "Do your duty."

         Oh, Christofo Columbo,
         Found here was solid ground-o,
         That stop-your-shoving, woman-loving,
         Son-of-a-gun, Columbo!

13. The sailors jumped into the surf,
     And shed their coats and collars,
  Columbo said, "The first one there
     Will get a hundred dollars."

         Oh, Christofo Columbo,
         Knew where he was bound-o,
         That woman-baiting, captivating,
         Son-of-a-gun, Columbo!

14. He settled down to stay awhile,
    But things were not so pretty,
    The sailors started getting drunk
    Which really was a pity.

    > Oh, Christofo Columbo,
    > Got to where he was bound-o,
    > That heavy-headed, always-dreaded,
    > Son-of-a-gun, Columbo!

15. One day they loaded him in chain,
    And shipped him back to Spain.
    Columbo said, "I'm done for good
    These doings give me a pain."

    > Oh, Christofo Columbo,
    > He proved the world was round-o,
    > That pioneering, persevering,
    > Son-of-a-gun, Columbo!

16. When Columbo got back to Sunny Spain,
    He told them of bonanzas,
    They answered him, "We notice, Wop,
    You ain't got no bananas."

    > Oh, Christofo Columbo,
    > He showed the world was round-o,
    > That poorly treated, badly cheated,
    > Son-of-a-gun, Columbo!

Clementine

As sung by Ralph Geddes

Chorus:

Oh, my darling, oh my darling, oh my darling Clementine!
Thou art lost and gone for ever, dreadful sorry, Clementine.

Light she was, and like a feather,
And her shoes were number nine,
Sardine-boxes, without topses,
Sandals were for Clementine.

Chorus

Drove she ducklings to the water,
Every morning just at nine,
Stubbed her toe upon a splinter,
Fell into the foaming brine.

Chorus

Ruby lips above the water,
Blowing bubbles soft and fine,
Alas, for me! I was no swimmer,
So I lost my Clementine.

Chorus

In a churchyard, near the canyon,
Where the myrtle doth entwine,
There grow roses, and other posies,
Fertilized by Clementine.

Chorus

Then the miner, forty-niner,
Soon began to peak and pine,
Thought he 'oughter jine' his daughter,
Now he's with his Clementine.

Chorus

In my dreams she oft doth haunt me,
With her garments soaked in brine,
Though in life I used to hug her,
Now she's dead I draw the line.

Chorus

When I Die

When I die, don't bury me at all,
Just pickle my bones in alcohol:
A scuttle of booze
At my head and shoes,
   And then my bones will surely keep.

One More Drink for the Four of Us

I was drunk last night,
   Drunk the night before;
Going to get drunk tonight
   If I never get drunk any more.

     'Cause when I'm drunk
       I'm as happy as can be:
     For I am a member
       Of the souse familee.

Glorious, glorious,
   One more drink for the four of us.
Sing glory be to hob there's no more of us
   For one of us could kill it all alone.

Sweet Rosie

Sweet Rosie Levinsky,
She was a blacksmith by birth.
She was tired of living
And decided to leave this old earth.
She tried dying by inches,
But finding that this was too hard,
She went out in the alley
Laid down and died by the yard. . . .

              (spoken) three feet.

The Foggy, Foggy Dew

For I am a weaver and I live all alone,
And I work at the weavers' trade,
And the only, only thing I ever did wrong
Was to woo a fair young maid.
I wooed her in the summer time, part of the winter, too,
And there were many, many times
That I held her in my arms,
Just to keep her from the foggy, foggy dew.

One night she came to my bedside
When I was fast asleep.
Oh, that pretty little maid came to my bedside
And there began to weep.
She wept, she cried, she damn near died,
Alas, what could I do? So come cuddle into bed
To that pretty maid I said,
And I'll keep you from the foggy, foggy dew.

Now I am a bachelor and I live with my son
And we work at the weavers' trade.
And every time that I look into his eyes,
He reminds me of that fair young maid.
They remind me of the summer time,
Part of the winter, too;
Of the many, many times I held her in my arms,
Just to keep her from the foggy, foggy dew.

A Catch

A hoss and a flea an' a little mice,
Settin' in the corner shootin' dice;
Hoss foot slipped and he sot on the flea,
Flea sang out, "That's a hoss on me."

The Ballad Of Captain Kidd

My name was William* Kidd, when I sailed, when I sailed,
   My name was William Kidd, when I sailed,
     My name was William Kidd,
     God's laws I did forbid,
And so wickedly I did, when I sailed.

My parents taught me well, when I sailed, when I sailed,
   My parents taught me well, when I sailed,
     My parents taught me well,
     To shun the gates of hell,
But against them I rebelled, when I sailed.

I'd a Bible in my hand, when I sailed, when I sailed,
   I'd a Bible in my hand, when I sailed,
     I'd a Bible in my hand,
     By my father's great command,
And I sunk it in the sand, when I sailed.

I murdered William Moore, as I sailed, as I sailed,
   I murdered William Moore, as I sailed
     I murdered William Moore,
     And laid him in his gore,
Not many leagues from shore, as I sailed.

I was sick and nigh to death, when I sailed, when I sailed,
   I was sick and nigh to death, when I sailed,
     I was sick and nigh to death,
     And I vowed with every breath,
To walk in wisdom's ways, when I sailed.

*Kidd's name was given as Robert in the original version.

The Ballad of Captain Kidd

I thought I was undone, as I sailed, as I sailed,
    I thought I was undone, as I sailed,
        I thought I was undone,
        And my wicked glass had run,
But health did soon return, as I sailed.

My repentance lasted not, as I sailed, as I sailed,
    My repentance lasted not, as I sailed,
        My repentance lasted not,
        My vows I soon forgot,
Damnation was my lot, as I sailed.

I spied the ships from France, as I sailed, as I sailed,
    I spied the ships of France, as I sailed,
        I spied the ships of France,
        To them I did advance,
And took them all by chance, as I sailed.

I spied the ships of Spain, as I sailed, as I sailed,
    I spied the ships of Spain, as I sailed,
        I spied the ships of Spain,
        I looted them for gain,
'Till most of them was slain, as I sailed.

I'd ninety bars of gold, as I sailed, as I sailed,
    I'd ninety bars of gold, as I sailed,
        I'd ninety bars of gold,
        And dollars manifold,
With riches uncontrolled, as I sailed.

Thus being o'er-taken at last, as I sailed, as I sailed,
    Thus being o'er-taken at last, as I sailed,
        Thus being o'er-taken at last,
        And into prison cast,
And sentence being passed, I must die.

Farewell, the raging main, I must die, I must die,
    Farewell, the raging main, I must die,
        Farewell, the raging main,
            To Turkey, France and Spain,
I shall never see you again, for I must die.

To Execution Dock, I must go, I must go,
    To Execution Dock, I must go,
        To Execution Dock,
            While many thousands flock,
But I must bear the shock, and must die.

Come all ye young and old, see me die, see me die,
    Come all ye young and old, see me die,
        Come all ye young and old,
            You're welcome to my gold,
For by it I've lost my soul, and must die.

Take warning now by me, for I must die, for I must die,
    Take warning now by me, for I must die,
        Take warning now by me,
            And shun bad company,
Lest you come to hell with me, for I die.

The Old Grey Mare

The old grey mare ain't what she used to be,
    Ain't what she used to be;
    Ain't what she used to be;
O, the old grey mare ain't what she used to be
    Twenty years ago.
Twenty years ago, twenty years ago!
O, the old grey mare ain't what she used to be
    Twenty years ago.

The Dying Hobo

As sung by Helen Ramsey

Beside a western water tank,
   One cold November day;
Sheltered by a box car
   The dying hobo lay.

His partner sat beside him
   And slowly stroked his head;
As he listened to the last words
   The dying hobo said.

"I'm going to a better land,
   Where everything is bright;
Where handouts grow on bushes
   And you sleep out every night."

"Where a man don't ever have to work,
   Or even change his socks;
And little streams of whiskey
   Come trickling down the rocks."

"Just tell my girl in Denver,
   Her face no more I'll view,
For I'm going to hop a fast freight
   And ride her right straight through."

His eyes grew dim, his head fell back,
   He'd sung his last refrain.
His partner hooked his coat and pants,
   And caught an eastbound train.

Way Down Yonder in the Cornfield

Some folks say that a nigger won't steal,
    'Way down, 'way down, 'way down yonder in the cornfield.
But I caught a couple in my cornfield,
    'Way down, 'way down, 'way down yonder in the cornfield.

. . . . .

    Forty miles from whiskey
    And sixty miles from gin.

    I'm leaving this damned country
    For to live a life of sin.

The Lamentable History of Frankie and Johnnie

As sung by altogether too many persons

There are countless verses to this indubitably American folk-song and most of them are, quite honestly, ribald and unprintable. I have no sympathy for those commentators who insist that it is the unnatural spawn of the Negro melody, "Frankie and Albert." Surely the infidelity of the lover does not make it Negroid. My conclusions are that the latter is an Afro-American variant of the genuine ballad which found great favor among the covered wagon pioneers and Civil War soldiers.

The verses given herewith for all their limitations tell the story. They will serve as a starting point for those who know but a few scattered verses and as a basis for controversy for Frankie and Johnnie fans.

32 The Lamentable History of Frankie and Johnnie

Arrangement by Clinton Jonas.

Frankie and Johnie were lovers. O my gawd how they could love, they swore to be true to each other, Just as true as the stars up above, He was her man.... but he done her wrong....

2. Frankie she was a good woman,
   And Johnnie he was her man.
   And every dollar Frankie made
   Went right into Johnnie's hand.
   He was her man, but he done her wrong!

3. Frankie she was a good woman,
   Just like everyone knows,
   She paid a hundred dollars
   For every suit of Johnnie's clothes.
   He was her man, but he done her wrong!

4. Frankie and Johnnie went walking,
    Johnnie in his brand new suit.
   "O, my gawd," said Frankie,
      "But doesn't Johnnie look cute?"
         He was her man, but he done her wrong!

5. Frankie went down to Memphis,
      She went on the morning train,
   She paid a hundred dollars,
      For Johnnie a watch and chain.
         He was her man, but he done her wrong!

6. Frankie lived down at the crib-house*
      Crib-house with only two doors,
   Gave all her money to Johnnie,
      He spent it on those call-house girls.
         He was her man, but he done her wrong!

7. Frankie and Johnnie, those lovers,
      They had a quarrel one day,
   Johnnie he up and told Frankie,
      "Bye-bye, Babe, I'm goin' away,
         I was your man, but I'm just gone!"

8. Frankie went down to the gin-mill,
      To get herself a glass of beer,
   She said to that great big bartender,
      "Have you seen my lovin' man around here?
         'Cause he is my man and he wouldn't do me wrong."

9. "Ain't goin' to tell you no stories,
      Ain't goin' to tell you no lie,
   I saw your man 'bout an hour ago
      With a hussy named Ella Fly:
         And if he is your man, he's doin' you wrong."

*Crib-house: bed-house or lodging-house.

10. Frankie went down to the hockshop,
    She didn't go there for fun.
    She pawned all her jewelry
        And bought a great big forty-four gun,
            For to kill that man who was doing her wrong!

11. Frankie went down to the call-house,
        She leaned on that call-house bell,
    "Get out of the way all chippies and fools
        Or I'll blow you straight to hell;
            I want my man who is doing me wrong."

12. Frankie looked over the transom,
        And there to her great surprise,
    Yes, there on a couch sat Johnnie
        A-lovin' up that Ella Fly.
            He was her man and he was doing her wrong!

13. The girls all said to Frankie,
        "Frankie, now don't you shoot."
    But Frankie pulled down on the trigger
        And the gun went roota-toot-toot,
            Into that man who had done her wrong!

14. First time she shot him he staggered,
        Second time she shot him he fell,
    Third time she shot him, O Lordy,
        There was a new man's face in hell.
            She'd killed that man, who had done her wrong!

15. "O, roll me over, sweetheart,
        O, roll me over slow,
    O, roll me over on my right side
        Where the bullets ain't hurtin' me so.
            I was your man but I done you wrong."

16. After she shot him she was sorry,
        And it wrang her poor heart sore,

  To see her loving Johnnie
   Stretched across that hotel floor.
    But he was her man and he done her wrong!

17. Frankie went down to the undertaker's,
  And ordered up a casket sound;
All lined with silks and satins—
  The best that could be found,
   To bury that man who had done her wrong!

18. Bring on your open barouches,
  Bring on your rubber tired hack.
Seven goin' down to the cemetery
  But there's only six a-comin' back.
   They're planting that man who had done her wrong!

19. "O, bring 'round a thousand policemen,
  Bring 'em around today,
To lock me in the dungeon
  And throw the key away.
   I shot my man who was doing me wrong."

20. "Yes, put me in that dungeon,
  Oh, put me in that cell,
Put me where the north-west wind blows
  From the south-east corner of hell.
   I killed my man who had done me wrong."

21. Frankie she said to the warden,
  "What are they going to do?"
The warden he said to Frankie,
  "It's the electric chair for you!
   You killed your man because he done you wrong."

22. The sheriff came 'round in the morning,
  He said it was all for the best;
He said her lover Johnnie
  Was nothin' but a gawdam pest.
   He was her man and he done her wrong.

23. Frankie she sits in her crib-house,
    Underneath the electric fan,
    Telling her little sister,
        To beware of the gawdam man.
            "He'll do you wrong, just as sure as you're born."

24. This story has no moral,
        This story has no end,
    This story only goes to show
        That there ain't no good in men.
            They'll do you wrong just as sure's you're born.

Just a Wee Doch-an-Dorris

Just a wee doch-an-dorris,
Just a wee drap that's a',
Just a wee doch-an-dorris'
Before we gang awa'.
There's a wee wifie waitin'
With a wee bairn or two:
For if you can say
It's a braw brecht,
Moonlecht necht:
Yer a' recht, that's a'.

Hail, Hail!

Hail, hail, the gang's all here,
So what the hell do we care?
What the hell do we care?
Hail, hail, the gang's all here,
So what the hell do we care now?

The Dying Fisherman's Song

'Twas midnight on the ocean,
   Not a street car was in sight;
The sun was shining brightly,
   For it had rained all that night.

'Twas a summer's day in winter,
   The rain was snowing fast,
As a barefoot girl with shoes on
   Stood sitting in the grass.

'Twas evening and the rising sun
   Was setting in the west;
And all the fishes in the trees
   Were cuddled in their nests.

The rain was pouring down,
   The sun was shining bright,
And everything that you could see
   Was hidden out of sight.

The organ peeled potatoes,
   Lard was rendered by the choir;
When the sexton rang the dishrag
   Someone set the church on fire.

"Holy smokes!" the teacher shouted,
   As he madly tore his hair.
Now his head resembles heaven,
   For there is no parting there.

I Had But Fifty Cents

As sung by James E. Harris

I took my girl to a ball last night, 'twas such a fan-cy hop, We stayed un-til the folks went home, the mu-sic it did stop; Then to a rest-au-rant we went, The fin-est on the street She said she was-n't hun-gry but this is what she'd eat:

2. A dozen raw, a plate of slaw, some fancy Boston roast,
   Some turtle stew, crackers, too, some soft-shelled crab on toast;
   Next she tried some oysters fried—her appetite was immense!
   She asked for pie! I thought I'd die, for I had but fifty cents!

3. After eating all of this she smiled so very sweet;
   She said she wasn't hungry at all, she wished that she could eat.
   But the very next order that she gave, my heart within me sank:
   She said she wasn't thirsty at all, but this is what she drank:

4. A brandy, a gin, a big hot rum, a schooner of lager beer,
   Some whiskey skins and two more gins did quickly disappear;
   A bottle of ale, a soda cocktail, she astonished all the gents!
   She called for more, I fell on the floor, for I had but fifty cents.

5. To finish up, this delicate girl cleaned out an ice cream can;
   She says, "Now, Sam, I'll tell mama you're such a nice young man."
   She said she'd bring her sister along next time she came, for fun;
   I handed the man my fifty cents, and this is what he done:

6. He broke my nose, he tore my clothes, he knocked me out of breath;
   I took the prize for two black eyes, he kicked me most to death;
   At every chance he made me dance, he fired me over the fence.
   Take my advice: don't try it twice, when you have but fifty cents.

I've Been Workin' on the Railroad

I've been workin' on the railroad,
    All the live long day:
I've been workin' on the railroad
    Just to pass the time away.
Don't you hear the whistle tooting?
    Rise up so early in the morn.
Don't you hear the foreman shouting?
    Dinah, blow your horn.

Little Brown Jug

My wife and I live all alone
  In a little brown hut we call our own,
She loves gin and I love rum,
  Tell you what, don't we have fun?

    Chorus:

  Ha, ha, ha, 'Tis you and me,
  Little brown jug don't I love thee?
  Ha, ha, ha, 'Tis you and me,
  Little brown jug don't I love thee?

If I had a cow that gave such milk
  I'd dress her in the finest silk,
Feed her on the choicest hay,
  And milk her forty times a day.

    Chorus

'Tis you that makes my friends my foes,
  'Tis you that makes me wear old clothes,
But seeing you are so near my nose,
  Tip her up and down she goes.

    Chorus

When I go toiling on my farm,
  Take little brown jug under my arm,
Set it under some shady tree,
  Little brown jug, don't I love thee?

    Chorus

Then came the landlord tripping in,
   Round top hat and peaked chin,
In his hand he carried a cup,
   Says I, "Old fellow, give us a sup."

Chorus

If all the folks of Adam's race,
   Were put together in one place,
Then I'd prepare to drop a tear
   Before I'd part with you, my dear.

Chorus

I Know Where They Are

If you want to find the Majors
   I know where they are,
      Yes, I know where they are.
If you want to find the Majors
   I know where they are,
Down in the deep dugout,
   I saw them, I saw them,
Down in the deep dugout,
   I saw them
      Down in the deep dugout.

I'm Full

I'm full, absolutely full,
But I know the country I was born in.
My name is Jock McGraw
And I dinna care a straw,
For I've a wee bit drappie
In the bottle for the mornin'.

Jesse James

From William H. Wells, New York

How the people held their breath
When they heard of Jesse's death
    And wondered how he came to die;
For the big reward
Little Robert Ford
    Shot Jesse James on the sly.

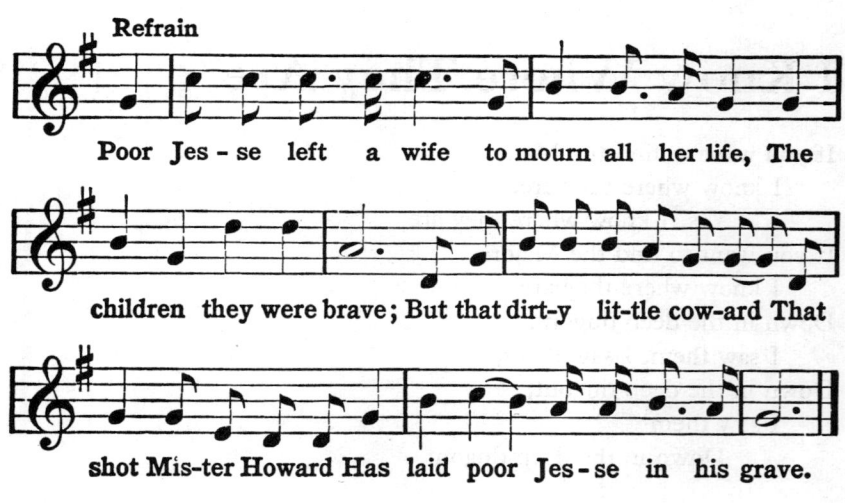

Poor Jesse left a wife to mourn all her life, The children they were brave; But that dirty little coward That shot Mister Howard Has laid poor Jesse in his grave.

Jesse was a man,
A friend of the poor,
    Never did he suffer a man's pain;
And with his brother Frank
He robbed the Chicago bank,
    And stopped the Glendale train.

Chorus

Jesse goes to rest
With his hand on his breast,
   And the devil will be upon his knees;
He was born one day
In the county of Clay,
   And came from a great race.

      Chorus

Men when you go out to the West,
   Don't be afraid to die;
With the law in their hand,
But they didn't have the sand
   For to take Jesse James alive.

      Chorus

Back and Side Go Bare, Go Bare!

This version, attributed to Bishop John Still, was a modernization of a twelfth-century ballad. It sounds as though it might find great favor at Oxford.

Back and side go bare, go bare!
   Both foot and hand grow cold;
But belly, God send thee good ale enough,
   Whether it be new or old.

I cannot eat but little meat,
   My stomach is not good;
But sure I think that I can drink
   With him that wears a hood.
Though I go bare, take ye no care,
   I nothing am a-cold.
I stuff my skin so full within
   Of jolly good ale and old.

Back and Side Go Bare, Go Bare!

Back and side go bare, go bare
    Both foot and hand grow cold;
But belly, God send thee good ale enough,
    Whether it be new or old.

I have no roast but a nut-brown toast,
    And a crab laid in the fire;
A little bread shall do me stead,
    Much bread I do not desire.
No frost nor snow, nor wind I trow,
    Can hurt me if I wold;
I am so wrapped, and thoroughly lapped,
    Of jolly good ale and old.

Back and side go bare, etc.

And Tib my wife, that as her life
    Loveth well good ale to seek,
Full oft drinks she, till ye may see
    The tears run down her cheek;
Then doth she trowl to me the bowl,
    Even as a maltworm should,
And saith, Sweetheart, I took my part
    Of this jolly good ale and old.

Back and side go bare, etc.

Then let them drink till they nod and wink,
    Even as good fellows should do;
They shall not miss to have the bliss
    Good ale doth bring men to:
And all poor souls that have scoured bowls,
    Or have them lustily trowled,
God save the lives of them and their wives,
    Whether they be young or old.

Back and side go bare, etc.

Fill the Flowing Bowl

Early eighteenth-century ballad.

He that drinketh strong beer and goes to bed right mellow,
Lives as he ought to live and dies a hearty fellow.

> *Chorus :*
> Come, landlord, fill the flowing bowl
>   Until it does run over.
> For tonight we'll merry be, merry be, merry be,
>   Tomorrow we'll get sober.

He that drinketh small beer and goes to bed quite sober,
Falls as the leaves do fall that die in dull October.

> *Chorus*

Punch cures the gout, the colic and the phthisic,*
And is to all men the very best of physic.

> *Chorus*

He that courts a pretty girl, and courts her for his pleasure,
Is a knave unless he marries her without store or treasure.

> *Chorus*

Now let us dance and sing and drive away all sorrow,
For perhaps we may not meet again tomorrow.

> *Chorus :*
> Come landlord, fill the flowing bowl
>   Until it does run over.
> For tonight we'll merry be, merry be, merry be,
>   Tomorrow we'll get sober.

*Tisic, a progressive wasting disease, especially pulmonary consumption.

Le Chef de Gare

Le chef de gare
Il est coucou,
Le chef de gare
Il est coucou,
Qui est coucou ?
Le chef de gare.
C'est que sa femme
Voulut—voulut—
Oh—ee. Oh—ee
Voulut—Voulut.

The Ballad Of Lydia Pinkham

As sung by John Fitzgerald

When we sing of Lydia Pinkham
    And how she loved the human race,
And how she sold her vegetable compound,
    And how the papers published her face,
          published her face!

O, Mrs. Brown could do no housework,
    O, Mrs. Brown could do no housework,
She took three bottles of Lydia's compound,
    And now there's nothing she will shirk,
          she will shirk!

O, Mrs. Jones, etc.
O, Mrs. White, etc.
O, Mrs. Green, etc.

Another version is

Mrs. Jones she had no children,
  And she loved them very dear.
So she took six bottles of Pinkham's—
  Now she has twins every year.

Chorus:

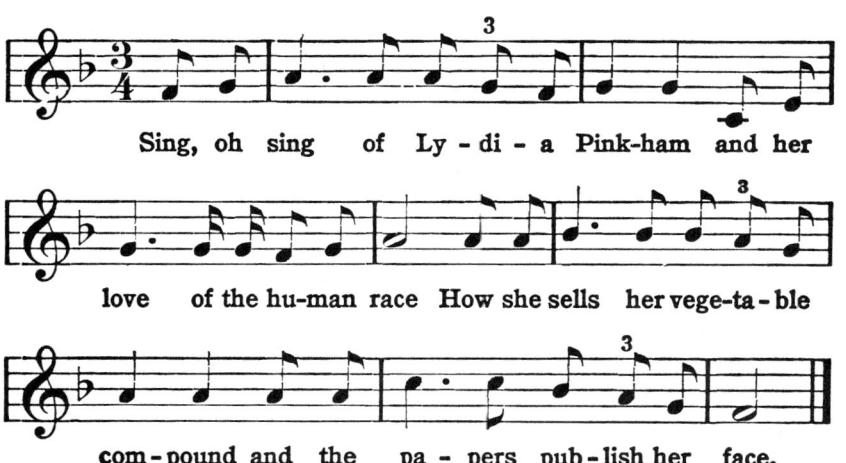

Sing, oh sing of Ly-di-a Pink-ham and her love of the hu-man race How she sells her vege-ta-ble com-pound and the pa-pers pub-lish her face.

Lottie Smyth ne'er had a lover,
  Blotchy pimples caused her plight;
But she took nine bottles of Pinkham's—
  Sweethearts swarm about her each night.

Railroad Bill

Rail - road Bill, Rail - - road Bill, He nev - er worked and he nev - er will, That bad Rail - road Bill.

Railroad Bill, mighty bad man.
Shoot all de lamps off de stan',
    That bad Railroad Bill.

Railroad Bill, so mean and so bad,
Took ev'ything the po' farmer had,
    That bad Railroad Bill.

Somebody went home an' tol' my wife,
All about—well, my pas' life,
    Wus that Railroad Bill.

Railroad Bill never had no wife,
Always lookin' for someone's life,
    That bad Railroad Bill.

I'm goin' home and tell my wife,
Railroad Bill tried to take my life,
    Yes, bad Railroad Bill.

Ol' Macmillan had a special train,
When he got there wus a shower of rain,
    Wus lookin' for Railroad Bill.

Ev'ybody tol' him he better go back,
Railroad Bill wus comin' down de track,
    Wus Railroad Bill.

Railroad Bill was the worst ol' coon,
Shot Macmillan by the light of de moon,
    Yes, that bad Railroad Bill.

Sheriff came a-knockin' at de do'
Said he was lookin' fo' me no mo',
    Lookin' for Railroad Bill.

Ten policemen all dressed in blue,
Comin' down the street two by two,
    Lookin' for Railroad Bill.

Ev'body tol' him he better go back,
Policemen comin' down de railroad track,
    An' a-lookin' for Railroad Bill.

Railroad Bill, a-waitin' at de tank,
Waitin' fo' de train called de Nancy Hank,
    In the mornin' jus' 'fo day.

Ol' Culpepper went up on Number Five,
Goin' bring him back dead or alive,
    That bad Railroad Bill.

Railroad Bill said befo' he died,
Goin' build a railroad fo' de hoboes to ride,
    Ride on, Railroad Bill.

First on de table, nex' on de wall,
Ol' corn whiskey cause of it all,
    Done lookin' fo' Railroad Bill.

Railroad Bill led a mighty bad life,
Always hookin' some other man's wife,
    That bad Railroad Bill.

The Morning After

A gilded mirror, a polished bar,
    A million glasses, straws in a jar:
A courteous young man, all dressed in white,
    Are my recollections of last night!

The streets were dirty and far too long,
    Gutters sloppy and policemen strong:
The slamming of doors in a sea-going hack;
    That's my recollection of getting back!

The stairs were narrow and hard to climb,
    I rested often for I'd lots of time:
An awkward keyhole, a misplaced chair,
    Told the folks plainly I was there!

A heated interior, a wobbly bed,
    A sea-sick man with an aching head:
Whiskey, beer, gin, booze galore,
    Were introduced to the cuspidor!

And with morning came bags of ice
    So very necessary in this life of vice;
And when I cooled my throbbing brain,
    Did I swear off and quit? No, I got soused again.

The Oregon Trail

As sung by Helen Ramsey

Way down yander in the Wahee Mountains,
   Where folks don't know about books nor countin's,
There lived a Zeke, an old galoot,
   And all he knew was how to shoot.
He had a girl and he would always tell 'er,
   Not to monkey with a city feller;
The city feller came without fail
   And old Zeke shot 'im on the Oregon Trail.

On the Oregon Trail, that's where he shot 'im;
On the Oregon Trail, they came and got 'im.
The city feller came without fail
And old Zeke shot 'im on the Oregon Trail.

Hezekiah had a lovely daughter,
   Never did a thing she hadn't oughter,
And married Zeke and they went alone
   Up in the mountains and built a home.

It wasn't long until the stork came flying,
   Brought a kid that was always crying.
The poor stork died he grew so frail,
   —Couldn't stand it on the Oregon Trail.

On the Oregon Trail that's where they killed 'im,
On the Oregon Trail a tomb they built 'im.
They dug his grave and on it wrote, "This poor bird was the family goat."
He carried kids until his back was broke on the Oregon Trail.

O'Slattery's Light Dragoons

You have heard of Julius Caesar and of great Napoleon, too,
And how the Cork militia beat the Turks at Waterloo.
But there's a page of glory that as yet remains uncut,
'Tis the immortal story of O'Slattery's mounted foot.

This gallant corps was organized by O'Slattery's oldest son,
A noble minded poacher with a double-breasted gun,
And many a head was broken, aye, and many an eye was shut
In learning to maneuver with O'Slattery's mounted foot.

Then down from the mountains came the squadrons and platoons,
Those four and twenty fighting men and a couple of stout gossoons.
The band was playing merrily those patriotic tunes
Secure that fame would gild the name of O'Slattery's light dragoons.

First they'd reconnoiter 'round O'Sullivan's old shabeen;
It used to be a chop-house, but we called it the canteen,
And there we saw a notice that the bravest heart unnerved:
All liquor must be settled for before the drinks are served.

So on we marched but soon again each warrior's heart turned pale,
For rising high forninst us we beheld the county jail.
And when the army faced about 'twas in time to find
A couple of policemen had surrounded it from behind.

"Across the ditch," our leader cried, "and take the foe in flank,"
But yells of consternation then arose from every rank;
For posted high upon a tree we very plainly saw:
Trespassers prosecuted in accordance with the law.

"Foiled again," cried O'Slattery, "here ends our grand campaign,
'Tis merely throwing life away to cross yon raging drain;
I'm not so bold as lions but I'm braver nor a hen,
And he who fights and runs away will live to fight again."

So back to the mountains went the squadrons and platoons,
Those four and twenty fighting men and a couple of stout gossoons.
The band was playing cautiously those patriotic tunes,
To gild the fame, tho' rather lame, of Slattery's light dragoons.

We reached the mountains safely tho' all stiff and sore with cramp,
Each took a neat of whiskey straight to dissipate the damp;
And when their pipes were loaded up O'Slattery up and said:
Today's immortal fight will be remembered by the dead.

"I never will forget," said he, "while this brave heart shall beat,
The eager way ye followed when I headed the retreat,
Ye've heard the soldier's maxim when desisting from the fight;
'Best be a coward for five minutes than a dead man all your life.' "

So there in the mountains rest the squadrons and platoons,
The four and twenty fighting men and a couple of stout gossoons.
They march no more so martially to patriotic tunes,
But all the same they sing the fame of O'Slattery's light dragoons.

Samuel Hall

As sung by the Editor

My name is Samuel Hall, Samuel Hall,
My name is Samuel Hall, and I hate you one and all;
   You're a gang of muckers all—
      Damn your eyes!

O, I killed a man 'tis said, so 'tis said,
O, I killed a man 'tis said and I smashed his bleeding head,
   And I left him lying dead—
      Damn his eyes!

So they put me into quod, into quod,
So they put me into quod with a bar and iron rod,
   And they left me there, by God—
      Damn their eyes!

O, the parson he did come, he did come,
O, the parson he did come and he looked so very glum
   As he talked of kingdom come—
      Damn his eyes!

O, the sheriff he came, too, he came, too,
O, the sheriff he came, too, with his little boys in blue
   Saying, "Sam, I'll see you through"—
      Damn his eyes!

I saw Nellie in the crowd, in the crowd,
I saw Nellie in the crowd and I shouted right out loud,
   "Say, Nellie, ain't you proud?"—
      Damn your eyes!

So a swinging up I'll go, up I'll go,
So a swinging up I'll go while you people down below
   Shout up, "Sam, I told you so."—
      Damn your eyes!

Down Among the Dead Men

Early eighteenth-century ballad attributed to John Dyer (1700–58).

Here's a health to the king and a lasting peace,
To faction an end, to wealth increase;
Come, let's drink it while we have breath,
For there's no drinking after death.
And he that will this health deny
Down among the dead men let him lie!

Let charming beauty's health go round,
In whom celestial joys are found,
And may confusion still pursue
The senseless women-hating crew;
And they that women's health deny,
Down among the dead men let them lie!

In smiling Bacchus' joys I'll roll,
Deny no pleasures to my soul;
Let Bacchus' health round briskly move,
For Bacchus is the friend of love.
And he that will this health deny,
Down among the dead men let him lie!

May love and wine their rights maintain,
And their united pleasures reign;
While Bacchus' treasure crowns the board,
We'll sing the joys that both afford;
And they that won't with us comply,
Down among the dead men let them lie!

It's the Sime the 'Ole World Over

As sung by Harrison Dowd, Provincetown, Mass., 1925

She was just a par-son's daugh-ter pure and un-styned was her nyme, First 'e 'ad 'er then 'e left 'er And the poor girl lost 'er nyme.

Chorus:

It's the sime the 'ole world over,
   It's the poor what tikes the blime;
It's the rich what gets the grivy,
   Aynt it all a bleedin' shime?

Then she went to London city,
   For to 'ide 'er 'orrid shime;
There she met another squire;
   Once agine she lost 'er nime.

Chorus

Look at 'im with all 'is 'orses,
   Drinking champigne in 'is club.
While the victim of 'is passions
   Drinks her guinness in a pub.

Chorus

'Ear 'im in the 'Ouse of Commons,
   Mikin' laws to put down crime;
While the womyun that 'e ruined
   'Angs 'er 'ead in wicked shime.

Chorus

See 'er in 'er 'orse and carriage,
   Drivin' d'ily through the park;
Though she's mide a wealthy marriage,
   Still she 'ides a brikin' 'eart.

Chorus

In their poor and 'umble dwelling,
   Where 'er grievin' parents live;
Drinkin' champigne that she's sent 'em,
   But they never can forgive.

Chorus

In a rose embowered cottage,
   There was born a child of sin.
But the baby had no father
   So she gently did him in.

Chorus

It's the Sime the 'Ole World Over II

There is an alarming number of variations of this little piece. Several versions found favor with the British forces during the war. An American soldier of the Seventy-Eighth Division, A. E. F., was heard singing the following:

'Ave you 'eard of Sally Carter,
Who should 'ave been Joe Johnsing's wife?
First 'e gets 'er into trou - bell,
Then he ups and tikes a knife.

"Ow, dear Joe," cries 'eart-broke Sally,
"I will be thy loving bride."
"The 'ell you, will," says Joe, and promptly
Sticks the blade in 'er inside.

Wot a 'orrid scene of terror
For to see 'er lying stiff!
Wot a funny way of ending
Just a lover's little tiff.

An' now 'e's riding in his carriage,
Passin' laws in England's nime,
While the victims of 'is passion
Creep awi' to 'ide their shime!

That Tattooed French Lady

As sung by Packey Leveson

Tune: My Home in Tennessee.

O I gi'e a shillin' to see
   That tattooed French lady.
Tattooed from head to knee
   She was a sight to see.
Right across her jaw
   Was the Royal Flying Corps;
On her back was the Union Jack,
   Now could you ask for more?

All up and down her spine
   Was a squadron all in line;
And all around her hips
   Was a fleet of battleships.
Right above one kidney
   Was a birdseye view of Sydney.
But what I liked best was across her chest,
   My home in Tennessee!

The Son of a Gambolier

I'm a rambling rake of poverty,
   From Tippery town I came.
'Twas poverty compelled me first,
   To go out in the rain;
In all sorts of weather,
   Be it wet or be it dry,
I'm bound to get my livelihood
   Or lay me down and die.

Chorus :

Then combine your humble ditties
As from inn to tavern we steer,
   Like every honest fellow
   I drinks my lager beer,
   Like every jolly fellow
   I takes my whiskey clear,
For I'm a rambling rake of poverty
The son of a son of a son of a son of a gambolier.

I once was tall and handsome,
   And was so very neat,
They thought I was too good to live,
   Most good enough to eat;
But now I'm old, my coat is torn,
   And poverty holds me fast,
And every girl turns up her nose,
   As I go wandering past.

Chorus

I'm a rambling rake of poverty,
   From Tippery town I came,
My coat I bought from an old Jew shop,
   Way down in Maiden Lane;
My hat I got from a sailor lad
   Just eighteen years ago,
And my shoes I picked from an old dust heap,
   Which every one shunned but me.

Chorus

Water Boy

As sung by James E. Harris

Water boy,
Where are you hidin'?
Ef you don' come
I'm gwine to tell yo' mammy.

Dere ain't no hammer
Dat's on dis mountain,
That rings like mine, boys,
That rings like mine.
Done bus' these rocks, boys,
From here to Macon,
All de way to the jail, boys,
Yes, back to the jail.

You, jack of diamonds,
You, jack of diamonds,
Now I know yo' of old, boy,
Yes, I know you of old.
You rob my pockets,
Yes, you rob my pockets,
You done rob my pockets
Old silver and gold.

Water boy,
Where are you hidin'?
Ef you don't come
I'm gwine to tell yo' mammy.

There Is a Tavern in the Town

As sung by Ralph Geddes

There Is a Tavern in the Town

Chorus (cont'd):

Adieu, adieu, kind friends, adieu, adieu, adieu,
I can no longer stay with you.
I'll hang my harp on a weeping willow-tree,
And may the world go well with thee.

He left me for a damsel dark, damsel dark,
Each Friday night they used to spark, used to spark,
And now my love, once true to me,
Takes that damsel on his knee.

Chorus

Oh! Dig my grave both wide and deep, wide and deep,
Put tombstones at my head and feet, head and feet,
And on my breast carve a turtle dove,
To signify I died of love.

Wal, I Swan

I run the old mill over here in Reubensville,
  My name's Joshua Ebenezer Frye;
I know a thing or two, just bet your boots I do,
  Can't fool me 'cause I'm too darn spry.
I've met your bunco men, always got the best of them;
  Once I met a couple on a Boston train.
They says, "How be you?" I says, "That'll do—
  Travel right along with your darned skinned game!"

Chorus:

Wal, I swan, I must be getting on;
  Git up, Napoleon, it looks like rain;
Wal, I'll be switched, the hay ain't pitched—
  Come in when you're over to the farm again.

I drove the old mare over to the country fair,
  Took first prize on a load of Summer squash.
Stopped at the cider mill coming over by the hill—
  Come home tighter than a drum, by gosh!
I was so darned full I gave away the old bull,
  Dropped both reins clean out on the fill;
Got home so darned late couldn't find the barn gate,
  Ma says, "Joshua, 'tain't poss-i-bill!"

Chorus

We had a big show here about a week ago,
  Pitched up a tent by the old mill dam;
Ma says, "Let's go in to see the side show—
  Just take a look at the tattooed man,"
I see a cuss look sharp at my pocketbook,
  Says, "Gimme two tens for a five?"

I says, "You darn fool, I be the constable—
  Now you're arrested sure as you're alive!"

      Chorus

I drove the old bay into town yesterday,
  Hitched her up to the railroad fence;
Tied her good and strong, but a train came along—
  I ain't seen the horse or the wagon sense.
Had to foot it home, so I started off alone,
  When a man says, "Hurry, your barn's on fire!"
Wal, I had the key in my pocket, you see,
  So I knew the cuss was a fool or a liar.

      Chorus

My son Joshua went to Philadelphia,
  He wouldn't do a day's work if he could;
He didn't give a darn about staying on the farm,
  What he's coming to ain't no good;
Smokes cigarettes, too, way the city folks do;
  Keep a-writin' home he's doing right well;
Seems kind of funny, but he's always out of money—
  Ma says the boy's up to some kind of hell.

      Chorus

Young Charlotte

Charlotte lived by the mountain side, In a wild and dreary spot, No other house for miles round, Beside her father's cot.

And yet on many a wintry night,
   Young swains were gathered there;
For her father kept a festive board,
   And she was very fair.

Her father loved to see her dressed
   Gay as any city belle;
She was the only child he had
   And he loved his daughter well.

One New Year's eve as the sun went down,
   Far looked her anxious eye
As along the snowy wintry road
   The merry sleighs passed by.

In the village fifteen miles away,
   Was to be a dance that night;
Though the air without was piercing cold
   Her heart beat warm and light.

How brightly beamed her laughing eyes,
    As the well-known voice she hear'd;
As driving up to the cottage door
    Young Charles and his sleigh appeared.

"Now, Charlotte, dear," her mother said,
    "This blanket 'round you fold;
It is a terrible night without;
    You'll catch your death of cold."

"Oh, no; Oh, no!" young Charlotte cried.
    And she laughed like a gypsy queen;
"To ride in blankets muffled up
    I never can be seen.

"My silken cloak is quite enough,
    You know 'tis lined throughout;
Besides I have my silken shawl
    To tie my neck about."

Her bonnet and her gloves put on
    She jumped into the sleigh:
And they drove down the mountainside
    And over the hills away.

There's life in the music of the merry bells,
    As over the hills they go;
Such a creaking sound the runners make
    As they crease the frozen snow.

With muffled faces tied about,
    Five miles at length were passed.
When Charles with few and shivering words
    Their silence broke at last.

"Such a dreadful night I never knew,
    My reins I scarce can hold."

Young Charlotte shivering feebly said,
  "I am exceeding cold."

He cracked his whip, he urged his steeds,
  Much faster than before.
And thus five more dreary miles
  In silence they passed o'er.

"How fast," says Charles, "the freezing ice
  Is gathering on my brow."
And Charlotte still more weakly said,
  "I'm getting warmer now."

And on they rode through the frosty air
  And the glittering cold starlight,
Until at last the village lights
  And the ballroom were in sight.

They reached the hall and Charles jumped out,
  And reached his hand for her.
Saying, "Why sit there like a monument
  That has no power to stir?"

He called her once, he called her twice,
  But she answered not a word.
He called for her again and again,
  But still she never stirred.

He took her hand in his. Oh, God!
  'Twas cold and hard as stone.
He tore the shawl from off her brow,
  Cold sweat upon there shone.

Then quickly to the lighted hall
  Her lifeless form he bore;
Young Charlotte was a frozen corpse,
  And danced she never more.

Then he sat himself down by her side,
  While bitter tears did flow.
He cried, "My own, my promised bride,
  I never more shall know."

He put his arms around her neck
  And kissed her marble brow;
His thoughts went back to where she said,
  "I'm growing warmer now."

'Twas then the cruel monster, Death,
  Was claiming her as his own;
Young Charlotte's eyes were closed,
  Poor Charles was all alone.

Then he bore her back to the sleigh,
  And with her he rode home;
And when he reached the cottage door
  Oh, how her parents mourned.

Her parents wept for their daughter dear,
  And Charles mourned in the gloom,
Till at last young Charles, too, died of grief,
  And they both rest in one tomb.

Young ladies, think of this dear girl
  And always dress aright,
And never venture so thinly clad
  Into the wintry night.

Whiskey for My Johnny

As sung by one who knew and loved his rye on board the Diesel Ship **Glenpool,** *August, 1915*

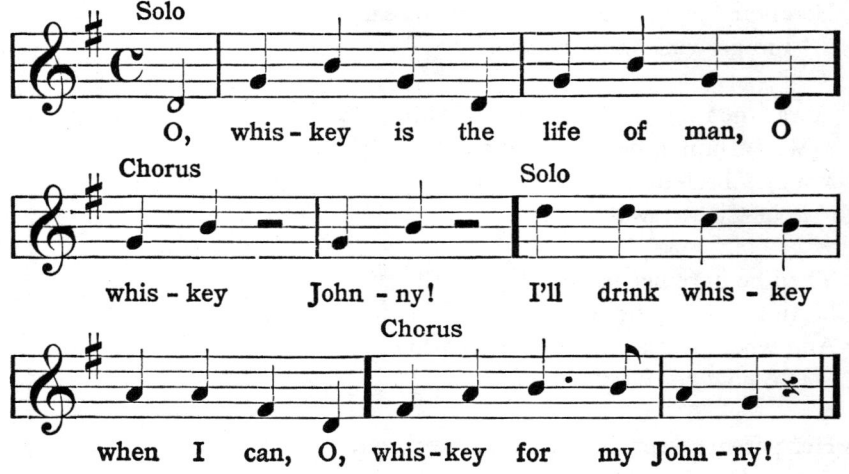

I'll drink whiskey when I can,
 O, whiskey, Johnny!
Whiskey from an old tin can,
 O, whiskey for my Johnny!

I drink it hot, I drink it cold,
 O, whiskey, Johnny!
I drink it new, I drink it old,
 O, whiskey for my Johnny!

Whiskey makes me feel so glad,
 O, whiskey, Johnny!
Whiskey killed my poor old dad,
 O, whiskey for my Johnny!

I Wish I Was Single Again

When I was single, Oh, then, Oh, then,
When I was single, Oh, then,
When I was single,
My money did jingle,
I wish I was single again, again,
I wish I was single again.

I married me a wife, Oh, then, Oh, then,
I married me a wife, Oh, then,
I married me a wife,
She's the plague of my life,
And I wished I was single again, again,
I wished I was single again.

My wife she died, Oh, then, Oh, then,
My wife she died, Oh, then,
My wife she died,
And then I cried,
To think I was single again, again,
To think I was single again.

I married another, the devil's grandmother,
I wished I was single again,
For when I was single,
My money did jingle,
I wish I was single again, again,
I wish I was single again.

Rolling Home

As sung by the crew of the S.S. Standard, *May, 1915*

Call all hands to man the cap-stan, See the ca-ble run down clear, Heave a-way, and with a will, boys, For old En-gland we will steer; And we'll sing in joy-ful cho-rus In the watch-es of the night, And we'll sight the shores of Eng-land When the gray dawn brings the light.

Call all hands to man the capstan,
  See the cable run down clear,
Heave away, and with a will, boys,
  For old England we will steer;
And we'll sing in jolly chorus
  In the watches of the night,
And we'll sight the shores of England
  When the gray dawn brings the light.

Rolling home, rolling home,
Rolling home across the sea;
Rolling home to dear old England,
Rolling home, dear land, to thee.

Up aloft amid the rigging,
  Blows the loud exultant gale,
Like a bird's out-stretched pinions
  Spreads on high each swelling sail;
And the wild waves cleft behind us,
  Seem to murmur as they flow,

There are loving hearts that wait you
   In the land to which you go.

Rolling home, etc.

Many thousand miles behind us,
   Many thousand miles before,
Ancient ocean heaves to waft us
   To the well-remembered shore.
Cheer up, Jack, bright smiles await you
   From the fairest of the fair,
And her loving eyes will greet you
   With kind welcomes everywhere.

Oh! Oh! Oh! It's a Lovely War!

Up to your waist in water,
Up to your eyes in slush,
Using the kind of language
That makes the sergeants blush;
Who wouldn't join the army,
That's what we all enquire,
Don't we pity the poor civilians
Sitting beside the fire?

    Chorus:

Oh! Oh! Oh! It's a lovely war,
Who wouldn't be a soldier, eh?
Oh, it's a shame to take the pay.

As soon as reveille has gone
We feel just as heavy as lead,
But we never get up till the sergeant
Brings our breakfast up to bed.

What do you want with eggs and ham
When you've got plum and apple jam?
Form fours! Right turn!
How shall we spend the money we earn?

    Chorus

When does a soldier grumble?
When does a soldier make a fuss?
No one is more contented
In all the world than us.
Oh, it's a cushy life, boys,
Really, we love it so;
Once a fellow was sent on leave
And simply refused to go.

    Chorus

Come to the cook-house door, boys,
Sniff at the lovely stew,
Who is it says the colonel gets
Better grub than you?
Any complaints this morning?
Do we complain? Not we.
What's the matter with lumps of onion
Floating around the tea?

    Chorus

Maid of Amsterdam

Maid of Amsterdam

Her eyes were blue, her cheeks were red,
   Mark well what I do say.
Her eyes were blue, her cheeks were red;
   A wealth of hair was on her head.
I'll go no more a-roving with you, fair maid.

Chorus

I put my arm around her waist,
   Mark well what I do say,
I put my arm around her waist;
   Says she, "Young man, you're in some haste."
I'll go no more a-roving with you, fair maid.

Chorus

I took that girl upon my knee,
   Mark well what I do say.
I took that girl upon my knee;
   Says she, "Young man, you're rather free."
I'll go no more a-roving with you, fair maid.

Chorus

Mademoiselle from Armentieres
(*Fragmentary*)

Mademoiselle all dressed in white, parlez vous. . . .
Mademoiselle all dressed in white, parlez vous. . . .
    Mademoiselle all dressed in black
    'Cause her Yankee didn't come back,
Hinky dinky, parlez vous.

O, the French they are a funny race, etc.
    They swipe your francs
    And lie to your face, etc.

The little marine he grew and grew, etc.
And now he's hugging and kissing 'em too, etc.

The little marine he grew and grew, etc.
And now he's part of the army too, etc.

Froggie, have you some very good wine? etc.
Fit for a bum right out of the line, etc.

Froggie, have you a daughter fine? etc.
Fit for a marine just out of the line, etc.

O, oui, I have a daughter fine, etc.
But not for a Yankee just out of the line, etc.

Froggie, have you a daughter fine, etc.
Fit for a doughboy up in the line, etc.

O, oui, I have a daughter fine, etc.
Fit for a Yankee up in the line, etc.

The little Yankee went over the top, etc.
He didn't know when the hell to stop, etc.

The little marine in love with his nurse, parlez vous. . . .
The little marine in love with his nurse, parlez vous. . . .
   The little marine in love with his nurse,
   He's taken her now for better or worse,
Hinky dinky, parlez vous. . . .

The Cowboy's Lament
*Version by Frank A. Lomax**

As I walked out in the streets of Laredo,
As I walked out in Laredo one day,
I spied a poor cowboy wrapped up in white linen,
Wrapped up in white linen as cold as the clay.

"Oh, beat the drum slowly and play the fife lowly,
Play the Dead March as you carry me along;
Take me to the green valley, there lay the sod o'er me,
For I'm a young cowboy and I know I've done wrong."

"I see by your outfit that you are a cowboy,"
These words he did say as I boldly stepped by.
"Come sit down beside me and hear my sad story;
I was shot in the breast and I know I must die."

"Let sixteen gamblers come handle my coffin,
Let sixteen cowboys come sing me a song,
Take me to the graveyard and lay the sod o'er me,
For I'm a poor cowboy and I know I've done wrong."

"My friends and relations they live in the Nation,
They know not where their boy has gone.
He first came to Texas and hired to a ranchman,
Oh, I'm a young cowboy and I know I've done wrong."

"Go write a letter to my gray-haired mother,
And carry the same to my sister so dear;
But not a word of this shall you mention
When a crowd gathers round you my story to hear."

"Then beat your drum slowly and play your fife lowly,
Beat the Dead March as you carry me along;
We all love our cowboys so young and so handsome,
We all love our cowboys although they've done wrong."

*From *Cowboy Songs* published by Macmillan Company.

"There is another more dear than a sister,
She'll bitterly weep when she hears I am gone.
There is another who will win her affections,
For I'm a young cowboy and they say I've done wrong."

"Go gather around you a crowd of young cowboys,
And tell them the story of this my sad fate;
Tell one and the other before they go further
To stop their wild roving before 'tis too late."

"Oh, muffle your drums, then play your fifes merrily;
Play the Dead March as you go along.
And fire your guns right over my coffin;
There goes an unfortunate boy to his home."

"It was once in the saddle I used to go dashing,
It was once in the saddle I used to go gay;
First to the dram-house, then to the card-house,
Got shot in the breast, I am dying to-day."

"Get six jolly cowboys to carry my coffin;
Get six pretty maidens to bear up my pall.
Put bunches of roses all over my coffin,
Put roses to deaden the clods as they fall."

"Then swing your rope slowly and rattle your spurs lowly,
And give a wild whoop as you carry me along;
And in the grave throw me and roll the sod o'er me,
For I'm a young cowboy and I know I've done wrong."

"Go bring me a cup, a cup of cold water,
To cool my parched lips," the cowboy said;
Before I turned, the spirit had left him
And gone to its Giver,—the cowboy was dead.

We beat the drum slowly and played the fife lowly,
And bitterly wept as we bore him along;
For we all loved our comrade, so brave, young and handsome,
We all loved our comrade although he'd done wrong.

The Face on the Bar-room Floor

By Hugh D'Arcy

'Twas a balmy summer evening, and a goodly crowd was there,
Which well-nigh filled Joe's bar-room, on the corner of the square;
And as songs and witty stories came through the open door,
A vagabond crept slowly in and posed upon the floor.

"Where did it come from?" someone said. "The wind has blown it in."
"What does it want?" another cried. "Some whiskey, rum or gin?"
"Here, Toby, sic 'em, if your stomach's equal to the work—
I wouldn't touch him with a fork, he's filthy as a Turk."

This badinage the poor wretch took with stoical good grace;
In fact, he smiled as tho' he thought he'd struck the proper place.
"Come, boys, I know there's kindly hearts among so good a crowd—
To be in such good company would make a deacon proud."

"Give me a drink—that's what I want—I'm out of funds, you know,
When I had the cash to treat the gang this hand was never slow.
What? You laugh as if you thought this pocket never held a sou;
I once was fixed as well, my boys, as any one of you."

"There, thanks, that's braced me nicely; God bless you one and all;
Next time I pass this good saloon I'll make another call.
Give you a song? No, I can't do that; my singing days are past;
My voice is cracked, my throat's worn out, and my lungs are going fast."

"I'll tell you a funny story, and a fact, I promise, too,
Say! Give me another whiskey, and I'll tell you what I'll do—
That ever I was a decent man not one of you would think;
But I was, some four or five years back. Say, give me another drink."

The Face on the Bar-room Floor

"Fill her up, Joe, I want to put some life into my frame—
Such little drinks to a bum like me are miserably tame;
Five fingers—there, that's the scheme—and corking whiskey, too.
Well, here's luck, boys, and landlord, my best regards to you.

"You've treated me pretty kindly and I'd like to tell you how
I came to be the dirty sot you see before you now.
As I told you, once I was a man, with muscle, frame and health,
And but for a blunder ought to have made considerable wealth.

"I was a painter—not one that daubed on bricks and wood,
But an artist, and for my age, was rated pretty good.
I worked hard at my canvas, and was bidding fair to rise,
For gradually I saw the star of fame before my eyes.

"I made a picture perhaps you've seen, 'tis called the 'Chase of Fame.'
It brought me fifteen hundred pounds and added to my name.
And then I met a woman—now comes the funny part—
With eyes that petrified my brain, and sunk into my heart.

"Why don't you laugh? 'Tis funny that the vagabond you see
Could ever love a woman, and expect her love for me;
But 'twas so, and for a month or two, her smiles were freely given.
And when her loving lips touched mine, it carried me to heaven.

"Boys, did you ever see a girl for whom your soul you'd give,
With a form like the Milo Venus, too beautiful to live;
With eyes that would beat the Koh-i-noor, and a wealth of chestnut
    hair?
If so, 'twas she, for there never was another half so fair.

"I was working on a portrait, one afternoon in May,
Of a fair-haired boy, a friend of mine, who lived across the way;
And Madeline admired it, and, much to my surprise,
She said she'd like to know the man that had such dreamy eyes.

"It didn't take long to know him, and before the month had flown
My friend had stole my darling, and I was left alone;
And ere a year of misery had passed above my head,
The jewel I had treasured so had tarnished and was dead.

"That's why I took to drink, boys. Why, I never saw you smile,
I thought you'd be amused, and laughing all the while.
Why, what's the matter, friend? There's a tear-drop in your eye.
Come, laugh like me; 'tis only babes and women that should cry.

"Say, boys, if you give me just another whiskey I'll be glad,
And I'll draw right here a picture of the face that drove me mad.
Give me that piece of chalk with which you mark the baseball score—
You shall see the lovely Madeline upon the bar-room floor."

Another drink, and with chalk in hand, the vagabond began
To sketch a face that might well buy the soul of any man.
Then, as he placed another lock upon the shapely head,
With a fearful shriek, he leaped and fell across the picture—dead.

Twenty Years Ago

As sung by Helen Ramsey

Twenty years ago today,
The yellow sun was settin'.
A soldier boy marched to the fray
And left his parents frettin'.
He said, "Good-bye, my mother dear,
I'm goin' off to fight,
If I'm not home tomorrow,
I may not be home tonight."

"Oh, mother, say good-bye for me
To little Mollie Humphrey,
I hear the bugles callin'
And I must fight for my country."

Yo ho for the land he loves so well,
He fought with a slide trombone.
The horn was too low,
And caught in his toe,
It tripped him and he fell.

"Who'll save the flag!" the general cried.
"I will," replied a stranger.
"Although I promised mother
I'd not go near any danger."
Our soldier boy jumped up and cried,
"You shall not go alone,
For I will accompany you
Upon my slide trombone."

A cruel cannon it came up
And shot his legs away;
But he kept rushin' onward
In the middle of the fray.

Yo ho for the land he loved so well,
He fought in his suit of blue.
Though only a musician,
It shows his ambition
For the land he loved so well.

Lasca

By Frank Desprez
Recited with gestures, by Fern Forrester Shay

I want free life, and I want fresh air,
And I sigh for the canter after the cattle,
The crack of the whip like shots in a battle,
The melee of horns and hoofs and heads
That wars and wrangles and scatters and spreads,
The green beneath and the blue above,
And dash and danger, and life and love,
And Lasca!

    Lasca used to ride
On a mouse-gray mustang close to my side,
With blue serape and bright-belled spur;
I laughed with joy as I looked at her!
Little knew she of books or of creeds;
An Ave Maria sufficed her needs;
Little she cared save to be by my side,
To ride with me and ever to ride,
From San Saba's shore to Lavaca's tide.
She was as bold as the billows that beat,
She was as wild as the breezes that blow;
From her little head to her little feet
She was swayed in her suppleness to and fro
By each gust of passion; a sapling pine,
That grows on the edge of a Kansas bluff,
And wars with the wind when the weather is rough,
Is like Lasca, this love of mine.
She would hunger, that I might eat,
Would take the bitter and leave me the sweet.
But once, when I made her jealous, for fun,
At something I'd whispered or looked or done,
One Sunday, in San Antonio,

To a glorious girl on the Alamo,
She drew from her garter a dear little dagger,
And sting of a wasp!—it made me stagger!
An inch to the left or an inch to the right,
And I shouldn't be maundering here tonight;
But she sobbed, and sobbing, so swiftly bound
Her torn *rebozo* about the wound,
That I quite forgave her. Scratches don't count
    In Texas, down by the Rio Grande.

Her eye was brown—a deep, deep brown;
Her hair was darker than her eye;
And something in her smile and frown,
Curled crimson lip and instep high,
Showed that there ran in each blue vein,
Mixed with the milder Aztec strain,
The vigorous vintage of old Spain.
She was alive in every limb
With feeling, to the finger tips;
And when the sun is like a fire,
And sky one shining, soft sapphire
One does not drink in little sips.

  .   .   .   .   .

The air was heavy, the night was hot,
I sat by her side and forgot—forgot;
Forgot the herd that were taking their rest,
Forgot that the air was close, opprest;
That the Texas norther comes sudden and soon,
In the dead of night or the blaze of noon;
That, once let the herd at its breath take fright,
Nothing on earth can stop the flight;
And woe to the rider and woe to the steed
Who falls in front of their mad stampede!

  .   .   .   .   .

Was that thunder? I grasped the cord
Of my swift mustang without a word.
I sprang to the saddle, and she clung behind,
Away! on a hot chase down the wind
But never was foxhunt half so hard,
And never was steed so little spared;
For we rode for our lives. You shall hear how we fared,
        In Texas, down by the Rio Grande.

The mustang flew, and we urged him on;
There was one chance left, and you have but one—
Halt, jump to ground and shoot your horse;
Crouch under his carcase and take your chance;
And if the steers in their frantic course
Don't batter you both to pieces at once,
You may thank your star; if not, goodby
To the quickening kiss and the long-drawn sigh
And the open air and the open sky,
        In Texas, down by the Rio Grande.

The cattle gained on us, and, just as I felt
For my old six-shooter behind in my belt,
Down came the mustang, and down came we
Clinging together, and—what was the rest?
A body that spread itself on my breast,
Two arms that shielded my dizzy head,
Two lips that hard on my lips were prest;
Then came thunder in my ears,
As over us surged the sea of steers,
Blows that beat blood into my eyes
And when I could rise—
Lasca was dead!

I gouged out a grave a few feet deep,
And there in earth's arms I laid her to sleep;
And there she is lying, and no one knows,
And the Summer shines and the Winter snows;

For many a day the flowers have spread
A pall of petals over her head,
And the little gray hawk hangs aloft in the air,
And the sly coyote trots here and there,
And the black snake glides and glitters and slides
Into a rift in a cottonwood tree;
And the buzzard sails on,
And comes, and is gone,
Stately and still, like a ship at sea.
And I wonder why I do not care
For the things that are, like the things that were,
Does half my heart lie buried there,
      In Texas, down by the Rio Grande?

'Ostler Joe

By George R. Sims

I stood at eve where the sun went down,
    By a grave where a woman lies,
Who lured men's souls to the shores of sin
    With the light of her wanton eyes;
Who sang the song that the siren sang
    On the treacherous Lorelei height,
Whose face was as fair as a Summer's day
    And whose heart was as black as night.

Yet a blossom I fain would pluck to-day
    From the garden above her dust—
Not the languorous lily of soulless sin,
    Nor the blood-red rose of lust—
But a sweet white blossom of holy love
    That grew in that one green spot
In the arid desert of Phryne's life,
    Where all else was parched and hot.

In the Summer, when the meadows
    Were aglow with blue and red,
Joe, the 'ostler of "The Magpie,"
    And fair Annie Smith were wed.
Plump was Annie, plump and pretty,
    With a face as fair as snow;
He was anything but handsome,
    Was the "Magpie's" 'ostler Joe.

But he won the winsome lassie;
    They'd a cottage and a cow—
And her matronhood sat lightly
    On the village beauty's brow.

Sped the months, and came a baby—
   Such a blue-eyed baby boy,
Joe was working in the stables
   When they told him of his joy.

He was rubbing down the horses—
   Gave them, then and there,
All a special feed of clover,
   Just in honor of his heir.
It had been his great ambition
   (And he told the horses so)
That the fates would send a baby
   Who might bear the name of Joe.

Little Joe, the child was christened,
   And like babies grew apace.
He'd his mother's eyes of azure
   And his father's honest face.
Swift the happy years went over,
   Years of blue and cloudless sky;
Love was lord of that small cottage
   And the tempest passed them by.

Down the lane by Annie's cottage
   Chanced a gentleman to roam;
He caught a glimpse of Annie
   In her bright and happy home.
Thrice he came and saw her sitting
   By the window with her child,
And he nodded to the baby,
   And the baby laughed and smiled.

So at last it grew to know him
   (Little Joe was nearly four),
He would call the pretty "gemplum"
   As he passed the open door.

And one day he ran and caught him,
    And in child's play pulled him in;
And the baby Joe had prayed for
    Brought about the mother's sin.

'Twas the same old wretched story,
    That for ages bards have sung;
'Twas a woman, weak and wanton,
    And a villain's tempting tongue;
'Twas a picture deftly painted
    For a silly creature's eyes,
Of the Babylonian wonders
    And the joy that in them lies.

Annie listened and was tempted—
    Was tempted and she fell,
As the angels fell from Heaven
    To the blackest depths of Hell.
She was promised wealth and splendor
    And a life of genteel sloth;
Yellow gold, for child and husband—
    And the woman left them both.

Home one eve came Joe, the 'ostler,
    With a cheery cry of "Wife!"
Finding that which blurred forever
    All the story of his life.
She had left a silly letter,
    Through the cruel scrawl he spelt,
Then he sought the lonely bedroom,
    Joined his horny hands and knelt.

"Now, O Lord, O God, forgive her,
    For she ain't to blame," he cried;
"For I ought to seen her trouble
    And a-gone away and died.

Why a girl like her—God bless her—
  T'wasn't likely as she'd rest
With her bonny head forever
  On a 'ostler's ragged vest."

"It was kind o' her to bear with me
  All the long and happy time;
So, for my sake please to bless her,
  Though you count her deed a crime.
If so be I don't pray proper,
  Lord, forgive me, for you see,
I can talk all right to 'osses,
  But I'm kind o' strange with Thee."

Ne'er a line came to the cottage
  From the woman who had flown;
Joe, the baby, died that Winter,
  And the man was left alone.
Ne'er the bitter word he uttered,
  But in silence kissed the rod,
Saving what he told his horses,
  Saving what he told to God.

Far away in mighty London
  Rose the wanton into fame,
For her beauty was men's homage,
  And she prospered in her shame.
Quick from lord to lord she flitted,
  Higher still each prize she won,
And her rivals paled beside her
  As the stars beside the sun.

Next she trod the stage half naked,
  And she dragged Art's temple down
To the level of a market
  For the women of the town.

And the kisses she had given
  To poor 'ostler Joe for naught
With their gold and precious jewels
  Rich and titled roués bought.

Went the years with flying footsteps
  While her star was at its height:
Then the darkness came on swiftly
  And the gloaming turned to night.
Shattered strength and faded beauty
  Tore the laurels from her brow;
Of the thousands who had worshipped
  Never one came near her now.

Broken down in health and fortune,
  Men forgot her very name,
Till the news that she was dying
  Woke the echoes of her fame,
And the papers in their gossip
  Mentioned how an actress lay
Sick to death in humble lodgings,
  Growing weaker every day.

One there was who read the story
  In a far-off country place;
And that night the dying woman
  Woke and looked upon his face.
Once again the strong arms clasped her
  That had clasped her long ago,
And the weary head lay pillowed
  On the breast of 'ostler Joe.

All the past he had forgiven—
  All the sorrow and the shame;
He had found her sick and lonely
  And his wife he now could claim.

Since the grand folks who had known her
    One and all had slunk away,
He could clasp his long-lost darling,
    And no man could say him nay.

In his arms death found her lying,
    From his arms her spirit fled,
And his tears came down in torrents
    As he knelt beside his dead.
Never once his love had faltered
    Through her sad, unhallowed life,
And the stone above her ashes
    Bears the sacred name of wife.

That's the blossom I fain would pluck today
    From the garden above her dust;
Not the languorous lily of soulless sin
    Nor the blood-red rose of lust,
But a sweet white blossom of holy love
    That grew in the one green spot
In the arid desert of Phryne's life,
    Where all else was parched and hot.

The Kid's Fight

Us two was pals, the Kid and me;
'Twould cut no ice if some gayzee,
As tough as hell jumped either one,
We'd both light in and hand him some.

Both of a size, the Kid and me,
We tipped the scales at thirty-three;
And when we'd spar 'twas give and take,
I wouldn't slug for any stake.

One day we worked out at the gym,
Some swell guy hangin' round called "Slim,"
Watched us and got stuck on the Kid,
Then signed him up, that's what he did.

This guy called "Slim" he owned a string
Of lightweights, welters, everything;
He took the Kid out on the road,
And where they went none of us knowed.

I guessed the Kid had changed his name,
And fightin' the best ones in the game.
I used to dream of him at night,
No letters came—he couldn't write.

In just about two months or three
I signed up with Bucktooth McGee.
He got me matched with Denver Brown,
I finished him in half a round.

Next month I fought with Brooklyn Mike,
As tough a boy who hit the pike;
Then Frisco Jim and Battlin' Ben,
And knocked them all inside of ten.

The Kid's Fight

I took 'em all and won each bout,
None of them birds could put me out;
The sportin' writers watched me slug,
Then all the papers run my mug.

"He'd rather fight than eat," they said.
"He's got the punch, he'll knock 'em dead."
There's only one I hadn't met,
That guy they called "The Yorkshire Pet."

He'd cleaned 'em all around in France,
No one in England stood a chance;
And I was champ in U.S.A.,
And knocked 'em cuckoo every day.

Now all McGee and me could think
Was how we'd like to cross the drink,
And knock this bucko for a row,
And grab a wagon load of dough.

At last Mac got me matched all right,
Five thousand smackers for the fight;
Then me and him packed up our grip,
And went to grab that championship.

I done some trainin' and the night
Set for the battle sure was right;
The crowd was wild, for this here bout
Was set to last till one was out.

The mob went crazy when the Pet
Came in, I'd never seen him yet;
And then I climbed up through the ropes,
All full of fight and full of hopes.

The crowd gave me an awful yell,
('Twas even money at the bell)
They stamped their feet and shook the place;
The Pet turned 'round, I saw his face!

My guts went sick that's what they did,
For Holy Gee, it was the Kid!
We just had time for one good shake,
We meant it, too, it wasn't fake.

Whang! went the bell, the fight was on,
I clinched until the round was gone,
A-beggin, that he'd let me take
The fall for him—he wouldn't fake.

Hell, no, the Kid was on the square,
And said we had to fight it fair,
The crowd had bet their dough on us—
We had to fight (the honest cuss).

The referee was yellin' "break,"
The crowd was sore and howlin' "fake."
They'd paid their dough to see a scrap.
And so far we'd not hit a tap.

The second round we both begin.
I caught a fast one on my chin;
And stood like I was in a doze,
Until I got one on the nose.

I started landin' body blows,
He hooked another on my nose,
That riled my fightin' blood like hell,
And we was sluggin' at the bell.

The next round started, from the go
The millin' we did wasn't slow,
I landed hard on him, and then,
He took the count right up to ten.

He took the limit on one knee,
A chance to get his wind and see;
At ten he jumped up like a flash
And on my jaw he hung a smash.

I'm fightin', too, there, toe to toe,
And hittin' harder, blow for blow,
I damn soon knowed he couldn't stay,
He rolled his eyes—you know the way.

The way he staggered made me sick,
I stalled, McGee yelled "cop him quick!"
The crowd was wise and yellin' "fake,"
They'd seen the chance I wouldn't take.

The mob kept tellin' me to land,
And callin' things I couldn't stand;
I stepped in close and smashed his chin,
The Kid fell hard; he was all in.

I carried him into his chair,
And tried to bring him to for fair,
I rubbed his wrists, done everything,
A doctor climbed into the ring.

And I was scared as I could be,
The Kid was starin' and couldn't see;
The doctor turned and shook his head,
I looked again—the Kid was dead!

Don't Go in them Lions' Cage Tonight, Mother

As sung by Lawrence Grant and W. D. Smith

To be half-recited, half sung in a cross between a childish treble and a whiskey tenor to any melody you can adapt to the words. It is quite effective at certain stages.

A lady once she had a lovely daughter,
   The lady was an actress on the stage.
She traveled with a troupe of awful lions,
   And each night she went in them lions' cage.
One night the daughter had a premonition
   That everything that night would not be right,
And so she told her mother in the kitchen,
   "Oh, don't go near them lions' cage tonight!"

Chorus:

   "Oh, don't go near them lions' cage,
     Dear mother, dear, tonight.
     Them lions am ferocious and might bite!
     And when they get them angry fits
     They'll chew you into little bits.
     Oh, don't go near them lions' cage tonight."

The lady laughed "ha ha!" she did not heed the warning
   That unto her her daughter she did give.
"Oh, no," she cried, "I do not fear them lions:
   Not one of them could make me cease to live."
She went into that cage of awful lions,
   Them lions were ferocious as could be.
"Alas," she cried, as one strode up and bit her,
   "I now recall what daughter said to me."

Chorus

"Oh, who will save my mother?" cried the daughter.
  "By lions she is being bit and et!"
"I will," replied a young man in the gallery;
  "I'll save your mother from them brutes, you bet!"
He went into that cage of awful lions,
  Of lion biting she was almost dead.
"Here is your ma," he said to her and kissed her;
  For he the daughter loved and soon did wed.

The High Barbaree

Heard on board the S.S. Standard *while afire off Yucatan, May 11, 1915*

The High Barbaree

The High Barbaree

"Aloft there, aloft!" our jolly boatswain cries,
Blow high, blow low, and so sailed we;
"Look ahead, look astern, look a-weather and a-lee,
Look along down the coast of the High Barbaree."

"There's nought upon the stern, there's nought upon the lee,"
Blow high, blow low, and so sailed we;
"But there's a lofty ship to windward, and she's sailing fast and free,
Sailing down along the coast of the High Barbaree."

"O hail her, O hail her," our gallant captain cried,
Blow high, blow low, and so sailed we;
"Are you a man-o'-war or a privateer," said he,
"Cruising down along the coast of the High Barbaree?"

"O, I am not a man-o'-war nor privateer," said he,
Blow high, blow low, and so sailed we;
"But I'm a salt-sea pirate a-looking for my fee,
Cruising down along the coast of the High Barbaree."

O, 'twas broadside to broadside a long time we lay,
Blow high, blow low, and so sailed we;
Until the "Prince of Luther" shot the pirate's masts away,
Cruising down along the coast of the High Barbaree.

"O quarter, O quarter," those pirates then did cry,
Blow high, blow low, and so sailed we;
But the quarter that we gave them—we sunk them in the sea,
Cruising down along the coast of the High Barbaree.

The Marines' Song

From the Halls of Montezuma
   To the shores of Tripoli,
We fight our country's battles,
   On the land as on the sea.
Admiration of the Nation,
   We're the finest ever seen,
And we glory in the title:
   The United States Marine.

From the Pest Hole of Cavite
   To the Ditch at Panama,
You will find them very needy
   Of marines. That's what we are.
We're the watch-dogs of a pile of coal,
   Or we dig a magazine.
Though our job lots are quite manifold,
   Who would not be a marine?

Our flag's unfurled to every breeze,
   From dawn to setting sun;
We've fought in every clime and place
   Where we could take a gun.
In the snows of far-off northern lands
   And in sunny tropic scenes,
You will always find us on the job,
   The United States Marines.

Here's health to you and to our corps,
   Which we are proud to serve:
In many a strife we have fought for life
   And never lost our nerve.

The Marines' Song

If the Army and the Navy
 Ever look on Heaven's scenes,
They will find the streets are guarded
 By the United States Marines.

This Book is Dedicated in General
to
The Society of the Forty Pious Friends
The International Bar Flies
The Amalgamated Order of Beer Shifters
The Barroom Boys and Girls
The Elite Order of Bung Starters
The Three Hours for Lunch Club
La Société des 40 Hommes et 8 Cheveaux
The Stowaways of New York
The Fraternal Order of Billy Goats
The Beachcombers of Provincetown
To Most of the Elks and Some of the Knights
To all Newspapermen Who Would be Great Writers
if They Could Leave the Stuff Alone
To That Great Army Who, Drunk or Sober, Love to Sing the
Old Songs of a Very Dear and Departed Era
And in Particular to
The Honorable Louis Bret Hart, of Buffalo.

Here's To Crime

The songs brought together in this second collection are, like their predecessors, snatched for the most part from a more beery and hilarious age. Some have the flavor of yesterday's bar-rag while others seem to have been brought into being by the ladies and gentlemen of the Anti-Saloon League. Some are frankly convivial and will serve as a goad to memories more tenacious than that of the editor. Others are merely the dolorous ballads sung by whiskey johnnies when in their cups. All of them have been tried out under the most exacting conditions and found not entirely wanting.

Since the first volume appeared there has been formed the Society of the Forty Pious Friends whose sole and main endeavor will be to seek out the songs of the dear, departed days and put them into practical use by keeping them alive for that future generation who, it is hoped, will throw off the shackles of sobriety that bind us. The society has endowed a completely equipped barroom from the swinging doors to the old third rail. The chief bartender is concert-meister and when the Board of Examination and Eligibility is completely and properly oiled he will give the word to the First Ivory Thumper. If the song proves acceptable under such conditions it will be placed in the society's repertory. For safety's sake the location of this laboratory must remain a secret.

Booze, under the present régime, has come out of the hell-holes and been given an honorable place in the American home. If the quality had only held up there would be but little room for complaint. The stuff they serve these days is terrible: there isn't a song in a boat-load. In the old days Father got his load at the corner. If it was that kind of a load he sang; if it wasn't he staggered a little. Mother knew by the tremolo of his voice or the footsteps on the stair that Father was not traveling on an even keel and herded the children out of the way until Daddy and his parcel were tucked into bed. Now Father is setting a bad example for the whole family by keeping the bottle under the kitchen sink where it will be handy. And when Mother feels a bit low she takes a shot of tiger milk and feels a lot better for a few moments. Joe, the eldest boy, who under normal conditions would be a tee-totaler until he was twenty-one, is not above pepping up his style with a jolt from the brew. Mamie, who is in business college, shows her young man that she knows how matters stand by slipping him a night-cap as he leaves.

Time was when the young man who occasionally took a drink called on his girl friend he was very careful to chew a clove or sen-sen to disguise his breath: he was careful not to let the aroma cross her nose. Today what happens? He calls on the girl and makes no effort to conceal the fact he has had a drink. The girl, if she is experienced, sets out a couple of glasses and a bottle of dry ginger ale. Has the young man appeared with nothing more than a breath? He is an inconsiderate fool, a stupid yokel, and the door is held open for him.

Travelers who have covered these states within the last few months tell us that nowhere have they found what is happily called "the dry sentiment." Is this phrase merely a device of the reformers and politicians? Well-known writers, several of them Englishmen, who have gone on extended lecture tours and who have been guests in the most American of homes, say they are always greeted with cocktails and that whichever way they turn they run into someone with a shaker who is just issuing dividends. In a very wide circle of friends the nearest to a total abstainer is one who is off the stuff temporarily for his health. The phrase, "No, I never touch a drop," went out with the Gibson girl.

What disturbs the ballad-monger is that there is less singing than ever. This may be due to the quality of the liquor we are throwing into us, for it is sodden stuff, or it may be due to the neighbors. What this country needs is a singing Lindbergh to make it "singing-minded" or a constitutional enactment absolutely prohibiting the singing of any but revival numbers. We need someone to lead us out of the boozy silence into which we have sunk. Those who have tried it know that a drink with a song is twice a drink.

A few of the hundreds who have written the editor since the first volume appeared seem to take it for granted that our home is one of hell's gaudy palaces, that we are a hell-roaring wild cat who each night makes the welkin ring with bawdy songs, that we are sold body and soul to the saloon interests. Such we regret is not the case though we must confess to a great longing to be all those things. Rather are we the good boy who has been celebrated in song by Lemuel F. Parton, the New York newspaperman:

> I have led a good life, full of peace and quiet,
> I shall have an old age, full of rum and riot;
> I have been a good boy, wed to peace and study,
> I shall have an old age, ribald, coarse and bloody.
>
> I have never cut throats, even when I yearned to,
> Never sang the dirty songs that my fancy turned to;
> I have been a nice boy and done what was expected,
> I shall be an old bum loved but unrespected.

FRANK SHAY

Provincetown, Mass.
June 1, 1928

Acknowledgments

It is a great pleasure to acknowledge the expert and valuable assistance given me by Judge Louis B. Hart, of Buffalo, Mr. W. W. Dean, of Indianapolis and others. Thanks are also due to Mr. Cardwell Thomson, H. Douglas Hadden, Robert Edwards, William B. Smith, John Held, Jr., D'Arcy Dahlberg, Miss Margaret Marshall, Harry T. Ramsey, Collins B. Reed, Mr. and Mrs. Edward J. (Tex) O'Reilly, James O'Reilly and Hal S. White.

The thanks of Miss Ramsey and myself must go to Cyril Mockridge for his patience and consideration.

Mr. Held's graphic illustrations again are used through the courtesy of *The New Yorker* and the Weyhe Galleries.

More Pious Friends and Drunken Companions

A Pack of Cards

As sung by John Held, Jr.

One night as I sat by my fire-side so wea-ry, And dream-ing of friends who were far, far a-way; My mem-o-ry brought me some that's sad and drear-y, Yet oth-ers came, too, that were cheer-ful and gay. When all of a sud-den I found my eyes rest-ing On some-thing that brought man-y scenes to my

The next scene I saw filled my heart with great pity,
It was a young man and his parents I knew,
'Twas their only son whom they'd sent to the city
To study and grow up a gentleman true,
A weekly allowance they thought would suffice him,
To live on the best and for studies to pay,
They knew not that evil companions enticed him
Away from his studies at poker to play!

> I saw him as he left his seat,
> He never thought his pals would cheat,
> Each time he played he met defeat,
> And still he called them pards.
> But there will come a reckoning day,
> And he will through this foolish play
> Bring sorrow in the old folks' way,
> All through that pack of cards!

The last scene of all I beheld with much sorrow,
For there was the scene of the gambler's black fate,
No thought had they got of the waking tomorrow
Though then they'd repent but to find it too late.
The bright gold was stacked by the side of each player,
The miser's black greed was in every man's heart,
As quickly the bets passed twixt backer and layer,
And Ruin was King in the Devil's slave mart!

> "I'll stake a hundred on this game!"
> "I'll go you, sir, I'll do the same."
> Who cares for misery and shame,
> As each his treasure guards?
> "You lie! I saw you turn that ace,"
> A smashing blow right in the face;
> A pistol shot, and death's disgrace,
> Was in that pack of cards!

The Roving Gambler

I am a rov-ing gam-bler, I've gam-bled all a-round, Wher-ev-er I meet with a deck of cards I lay my mon-ey down.

I've gambled down in Washington and I've gambled over in Spain;
I am on my way to Georgia to knock down my last game.

I had not been in Washington many more weeks than three,
Till I fell in love with a pretty little girl and she fell in love with me.

She took me in her parlor, she cooled me with her fan,
She whispered low in her mother's ears, "I love this gambling man."

"Oh daughter, Oh dear daughter, how could you treat me so,
To leave your dear old mother and with a gambler go?"

"Oh mother, Oh dear mother, you know I love you well,
But the love I hold for this gambling man no human tongue can tell.

"I wouldn't marry a farmer, for he's always in the rain;
The man I want is a gambling man who wears the big gold chain.

"I wouldn't marry a blacksmith, for he's always in the dirt;
For the man I want is the gambling man who wears a ruffled shirt.

"I wouldn't marry a doctor, for he is always gone from home;
All I want is the gambling man, for he won't leave me alone.

"I wouldn't marry a railroad man, and this is the reason why:
I never saw a railroad man that wouldn't tell his wife a lie.

"I hear the train a-coming, she's coming 'round the curve,
Whistling and a-blowing and straining every nerve.

"Oh mother, oh dear mother, I'll tell you if I can;
If you ever see me coming back again I'll be with the gambling man."

"I've gambled down in Washington and I've gambled over in Spain;
I am on my way to Georgia to knock down my last game."

Australian Highwayman's Song

As sung by Margaret Marshall

Australian Highwayman's Song

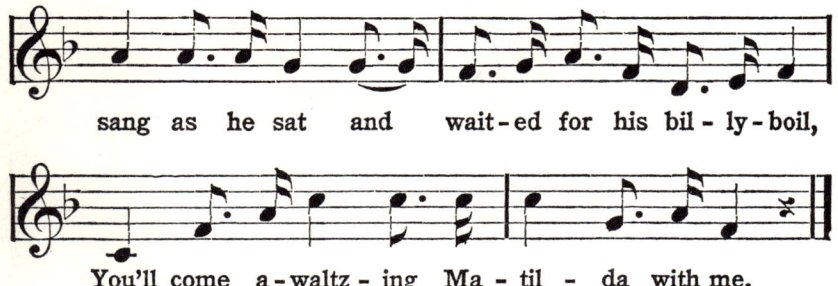

sang as he sat and wait-ed for his bil-ly-boil,
You'll come a-waltz-ing Ma-til-da with me.

Down came a jumbok to drink at the billy-bong,
Up jumped the swag-man and shot it with glee,
And he sang as he stuffed that jumbok in his tucker-bag,
"You'll come a-waltzing Matilda with me."

Chorus :

Waltzing Matilda, waltzing Matilda,
You'll come waltzing Matilda with me,
And he sang as he stuffed that jumbok in his tucker-bag,
"You'll come a-waltzing Matilda with me."

Up rode the stockman mounted on his thoroughbred,
Up rode the troopers, one, two, three,
"Where is the jumbok you have in your tucker-bag?
"You'll come a-waltzing Matilda with me."

Chorus :

Waltzing Matilda, waltzing Matilda,
You'll come waltzing Matilda with me,
"Where is the jumbok you have in your tucker-bag?
You'll come a-waltzing Matilda with me."

Up jumped the swag-man, leaped into the billy-bong,
"You'll never catch me alive," said he.

> (Slowly)
> And his ghost may be heard as you pass by the billy-bong,
> (Fast)
> "You'll come a-waltzing Matilda with me."

Chorus :

> Waltzing Matilda, waltzing Matilda,
> You'll come waltzing Matilda with me,
> (Slowly)
> And his ghost may be heard as you pass by the billy-bong,
> (Fast)
> "You'll come a-waltzing Matilda with me,

GLOSSARY

Swagman, highwayman. Billy-bong, brook. Billy-boil, coffee. Jumbok, lamb.

Our Gude-Man

Our gude-man cam' hame at e'en,
    And hame cam' he;
And there he saw a saddle-horse,
    Whaur nae horse should be.
"Oh, how cam' this horse here,
    How can this be?
How cam' this horse here,
    Without the leave of me?"
    "A horse?" quo' she,
    "Ay, a horse," quo' he.
"Ye auld blind doited carle,
    Blinder mat ye be!
'Tis naething but a milk-cow
    My minnie sent to me."
    "A milk-cow!" quo' he,
    "Ay, a milk-cow," quo' she.

"Far ha'e I ridden,
  And meikle ha'e I seen;
But a saddle on a cow's back
  Saw I never nane!"

Our gude-man cam' hame at e'en,
  And hame cam' he;
He spied a pair o' jack-boots,
  Whaur nae boots should be.
"What's this now, gude-wife?
  What's this I see?
How cam' these boots here,
  Without the leave o' me?"
    "Boots?" quo' she,
    "Ay, boots," quo' he.
"Shame fa' your cuckold face,
  And ill mat ye see!
It's but a pair o' water-stoups
  The cooper sent to me."
    "Water-stoups!" quo' he.
    "Ay, water-stoups," quo' she.
"Far ha'e I ridden,
  And farer ha'e I gane;
But siller spurs on water stoups
  Saw I never nane!"

Our gude-man cam' hame at e'en,
  And hame cam' he;
And there he saw a sword,
  Whaur nae sword should be.
"What's this now, gude-wife?
  What's this I see?
Oh, how cam' this sword here,
  Without the leave o' me?"
    "A sword?" quo' she.
    "Ay, a sword," quo' he.
"Shame fa' your cuckold face,

And ill mat ye see!
It's but a parritch spurtle
　My minnie sent to me.
　　"A spurtle?" quo' he.
　　"Ay, a spurtle," quo' she.
"Weel far ha'e I ridden,
　And meikle ha'e I seen;
But silver-handled spurtles
　Saw I never nane!"

Our gude-man cam' hame at e'en,
　And hame cam' he;
There he spied a pouthered wig,
　Whaur nae wig should be.
"What's this now, gude-wife?
　What's this I see?
How cam' this wig here,
　Without the leave o' me?"
　　"A wig?" quo' she.
　　"Ay, a wig," quo' he.
"Shame fa' your cuckold face,
　And ill mat ye see!
'Tis naething but a clockin' hen
　My minnie sent to me.
　　"A clockin' hen?" quo' he.
　　"Ay, a clockin' hen," quo' she.
"Far ha'e I ridden,
　And meikle ha'e I seen;
But pouther on a clockin' hen
　Saw I never nane!"

Our gude-man cam' hame at e'en,
　And hame cam' he;
And there he saw a riding-coat,
　Whaur nae coat shoud be.
"Oh, how cam' this coat here?
　How can this be?

How cam' this coat here,
   Without the leave o' me?"
     "A coat?" quo' she.
     "Ay, a coat," quo' he.
"Ye auld blind dotard carle,
   Blinder mat ye be!
It's but a pair o' blankets
   My minnie sent to me."
     "Blankets?" quo' he.
     "Aye, blankets," quo' she.
"Far ha'e I ridden,
   And meikle ha'e I seen;
But buttons upon blankets
   Saw I never nane!"

Bed went our gude-man.
   And bed went he;
And there he spied a sturdy man,
   Whaur nae man should be.
     "How cam' this man here?
     How can this be?
How cam' this man here,
   Without the leave o' me?"
     "A man?" quo' she.
     "Ay, a doited man," quo' he.
"Puir blind body!
   And blinder mat ye be!
It's a new milking-maid
   My minnie sent to me."
     "A maid?" quo' he.
     "Ay, a maid," quo' she.
"Far ha'e I ridden
   And meikle ha'e I seen;
But lang-bearded milking-maids
   Saw I never nane!"

Down in Dear Old Greenwich Village

As sung by Bobby Edwards

The only example of folk-song building to come to the editor's immediate attention is the following national anthem of New York's bohemia. Back in the old days when the Village began and ended at Polly's, when certain now distinguished men and women of letters were known as Oney, Theo, Jig, Sue and Vincent; when other names that are now known across the continent were just so many boys and girls struggling for recognition while living in garrets and basements and the editor had a beautiful hall-bedroom overlooking Washington Square for two dollars a week, the following ballad had its beginnings. Bobby Edwards, the last of the troubadours, gave it a prominent place in his repertory and later put it on paper. It is now so much his that the fullest credit must be given him. Nevertheless it is an indubitable folk-ballad in its origin and the first I ever heard sing it was George Baker, one evening at the aforesaid Polly's.

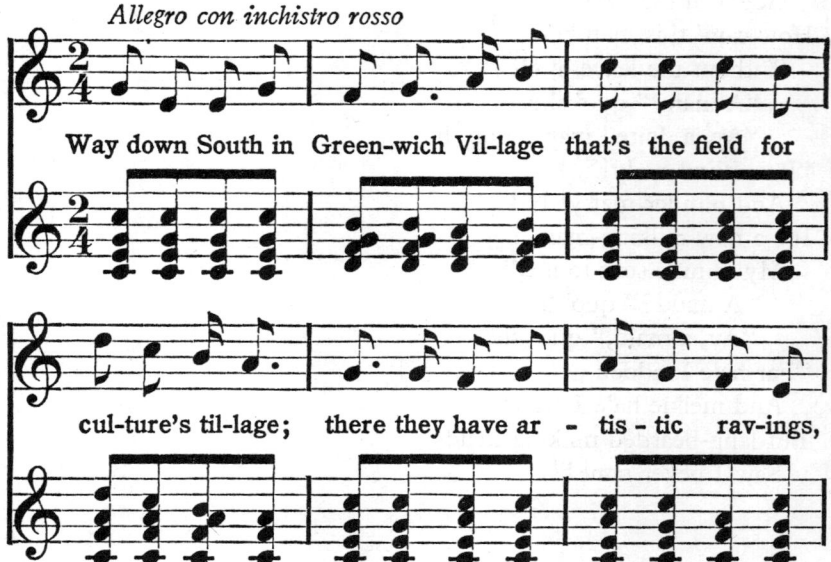

Down in Dear Old Greenwich Village

Down in dear old Greenwich Village,
   There they wear no fancy frillage,
For the ladies of the square
   All wear smocks and bob their hair.
There they do not think it shocking
   To wear stencils for a stocking,
That saves the laundry bills
   In Washington Square.

Way down South in Greenwich Village,
   Where the spinsters come for thrillage,

There they speak of "sex relations,"
    With the sordid Slavic nations.
'Neath the guise of feminism,
    Dodging social ostracism,
They get away with much
    In Washington Square.

Way down South in Greenwich Village,
    Where they all consume distillage,
Where the fashion illustrators
    Flirt with interior decorators.
There the cheap Bohemian fakirs
    And the boys from Wanamaker's
Gather "atmosphere"
    In Washington Square.

Way down South in Greenwich Village,
    Where the brains amount to nillage,
Where the girls are unconventional,
    And the men are unintentional.
There the girls are self-supporting,
    There the ladies do the courting,
The ladies buy the "eats"
    In Washington Square.

Way down South in Greenwich Village,
    Comes a bunch of Uptown Swillage,
Folks from Lenox Subway Stations
    Come with lurid expectations.
There the Village informalities
    Are construed as abnormalities
By the boobs that visit Sheridan Square.

The Wreck of the Old 97

They give him his orders at Monroe, Virginia,
Saying, "Pete, you are away behind time;
This is not Thirty-eight, but it's old Ninety-seven,
You must put her in Center on time."

He looked around and says to his black greasy fireman,
"Just shovel in a little more coal:
And when we cross that White Oak Mountain,
You can watch old Ninety-seven roll."

It's a mighty rough road from Lynchburg to Danville
And a line on a three-mile grade;
It was on that grade he lost his average,
And you see what a jump he made.

He was going down-grade making ninety miles an hour,
When his whistle broke into a scream.
He was found in the wreck with his hand on the throttle
And was scalded to death with the steam.

Now, ladies, you must take warning
From this time now on:
Never speak harsh words to your true love and husband
He may leave you and never return.

The Female Smuggler

Now, in sailor's clothing swell Jane did go,
Dressed like a sailor from top to toe;
Her aged father was the only care
Of this female smuggler,
    Of this female smuggler
    Who never did despair.

With her pistols loaded she went aboard.
And by her side hung a glittering sword,
In her belt two daggers; well armed for war
Was this female smuggler,
    Was this female smuggler,
    Who never feared a scar.

Now they had not sail-ed far from the land,
When a strange sail brought them to a stand.
"These are sea robbers," this maid did cry,
"But the female smuggler,
    But the female smuggler,
    Will conquer or will die."

Alongside, then, this strange vessel came.
"Cheer up," cried Jane, "we will board the same;
We'll run all chances to rise or fall,"
Cried this female smuggler,
    Cried this female smuggler,
    Who never feared a ball.

Now they killed those pirates and took their store,
And soon returned to Old England's shore.
With a keg of brandy she walked along,
Did this female smuggler,
    Did this female smuggler,
    Who sweetly sang a song.

Now they were followed by the blockade,
Who in irons strong did put this young maid.
But when they brought her to be tried,
This young female smuggler,
> This young female smuggler
> Stood dressed like a bride.

Their commodore against her appeared,
And for her life she greatly feared.
When he did find to his great surprise
'Twas a female smuggler,
> 'Twas a female smuggler
> Had fought him in disguise.

He to the judge and jury said,
"I cannot prosecute this maid,
Pardon for her on my knees I crave,
For this female smuggler,
> For this female smuggler
> So valiant and so brave."

Then this commodore to her father went,
To gain her hand he asked his consent.
His consent he gained, so the commodore
And the female smuggler,
> And the female smuggler
> Are one for evermore.

O, Give Me a Home Where the Buffalo Roam

As sung by Harry T. Ramsey

O, Give Me a Home Where the Buffalo Roam

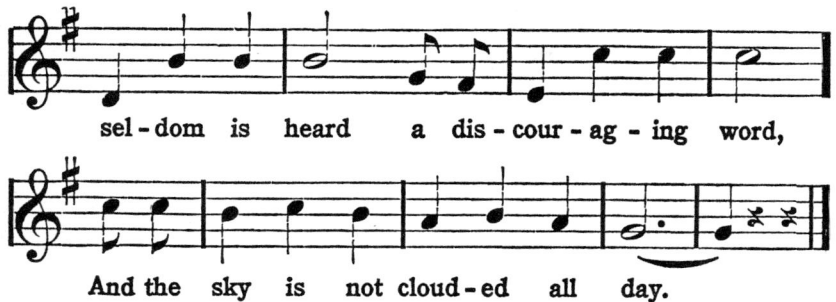

seldom is heard a discouraging word,
And the sky is not clouded all day.

O, give me a gale on the Solomon vale,
  Where life's stream joyfully flows,
On the banks of the Beaver where seldom, if ever,
  Any poisonous herbage doth grow.

Chorus

O, give me a land where the bright diamond sand
  Lies by the glittering stream,
Where glideth along, the graceful white Swan,
  Like a maid in her heavenly dream.

Chorus

Ofttimes at night, when summers are bright,
  By the light of twinkling stars,
I've stood here amazed, and asked as I gazed,
  If their glory exceeds that of ours.

Chorus

Heenan and Sayers

It was on the sixteenth day of April that they agreed to fight,
The money was all put up and everything was right,
But Heenan was arrested and brought to the county jail,
Where he was held to keep the peace under three hundred bail.

His friends went quickly there and they did bail him out,
He was forced to change his training ground and take another route;
They thought for to discourage him, so as to prevent the mill,
But having a brave heart in him, swore that Sayers' blood he'd spill.

To see those heroes in the ring it would make your heart feel gay,
Each wore a smile upon his face in honor of the day:
The spectators say they were eager those champions for to see,
For they both said that they'd either die or gain the victory.

Time was called, they both stood up, the excitement it was great,
To see those champions seeking to seal each other's fate;
Sayers he made a left-hand punch at Heenan's pretty face,
Who quickly dodged and with a blow laid Tommy near a case.

But when the second round came on the Briton was up to time,
Heenan made a pass at him, which slightly bruised his dial;
His friends they began to cheer, which made Sayers feel sad,
For he thought that he'd easily win, which would make the Yankees mad.

Sayers was up to time again, and his face it bore a smile.
Heenan made a pass at him, which slightly bruised his dial;
He made a terrific right-hand punch, which got on Heenan's jowl,
But quickly a sledge-hammer blow caused Sayers for to howl.

A look of melancholy was upon each Briton's face;
They thought that Sayers would get whipped and to England be a
    disgrace;

But then he got a handsome blow on brave Heenan's nob,
Their faces bore a smile again, and the betting on Sayers was odd.

Time was called, they both were up to toe the scratch once more,
Sayers got home on Heenan's mug, which made the Britons roar;
Heenan followed quickly up, and as Sayers turned around,
He met him with a right-hand blow which sprawled him on the ground.

Bold Sayers was up to time again, and he looked very bad;
Heenan looked as fresh again, which made the Britons mad;
They had a little false sparring, then at each other did gaze,
When Heenan sprawled him out again, which did the bulls amaze.

Then the cheers and bawls of Heenan's friends would make your heart feel gay;
For they were sure, they had no doubt, but he would gain the day:
The friends of Sayers began to think that he would soon give in,
And to think their champion would get beat it caused them to grin.

The fight was drawing to a close, the excitement growing worse,
The friends of Heenan they did cheer, and of Sayers they did curse,
The bulls were sure that Heenan would win, which caused them all to fret,
For every cent that they were worth on Sayers it was bet.

But then the thirty-seventh round came on to be the last,
The Briton's friends they plainly saw their man was failing fast;
When Heenan gave him another blow, which made them feel forlorn—
The Briton's friends jumped in the ring and said the fight was drawn.

But Heenan called on Sayers again to come and fight it out,
But he was so badly punished he could scarcely open his mouth:
Heenan said: "The fight is mine—and stood upon his ground—
Saying: "I am the champion of the world, in the thirty-seventh round."

Rio Grande

The an-chor is weighed and the sails they are set,

A - way ... Ri - o! ... The maids we are leav-ing we'll

nev - er for - get, For we're bound for the Ri - o Grande,

And a - way, ... Ri - o! ... Aye ... Ri -

o! ... Far we're bound for the Ri - o Grande.

So it's pack up your donkey and get under way,
    Away, Rio!
The girls we are leaving can take half our pay,

Chorus

We'll sing as we heave to the maidens we leave
    Away, Rio!
And you who are listening, good-bye to you,

        Chorus

Come heave up the anchor, let's get it aweigh
    Away, Rio!
It's got a firm hold, so heave steady, I say,

        Chorus

False Henry

Just a year ago tonight, mother, how sorrowful were we,
When sister May was taken, upon her wedding day;
O, mother, dearest mother, how much better it would have been for me,
Could I have died just like her, in my innocence and glee.

Just a year ago tonight, mother, I went down to a ball,
I went with my dear Henry, and danced with him till dawn;
There was not another maiden, with a lighter heart than mine,
But tonight I lie here dying, a mother, but no wife.

There will be a dance tonight, mother, and crowded it will be,
And I know that he will be with them, and he will think of me;
I own I love dear Henry, much better than I do life,
But tonight I lay here dying, a mother, but no wife.

Take this ring from off my finger, where he placed it long ago,
Give it to him with a blessing, and in joy let him go;
Just tell him I'll forgive him, for my sorrow and his sin;
Raise the curtains higher, dear mother, for my eyes are growing dim.

Here is my baby boy, mother, take and raise him up for me,
And give him food and plenty as you always did for me;
Then goodby, mother dearest, and you, my baby boy,
And you, my false young Henry, and she bade her last farewell.

The Charming Young Widow
I Met on the Train

The Charming Young Widow I Met on the Train

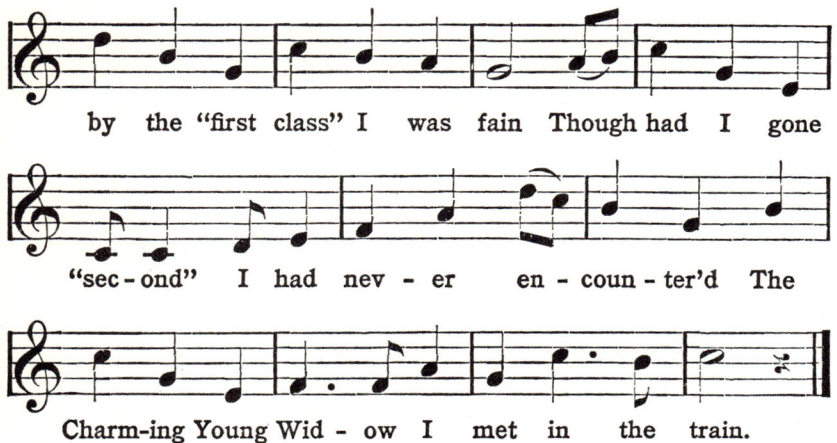

by the "first class" I was fain Though had I gone
"sec-ond" I had nev-er en-coun-ter'd The
Charm-ing Young Wid-ow I met in the train.

Now scarce was I seated within the compartment
Before a fresh passenger entered the door:
'Twas a female, a young one, and dressed in deep mourning,
An infant in long clothes she gracefully bore.
A white cap surrounded a face, oh, so lovely!
I never shall look on one like it again.
I fell deep in love over-head in a moment
With the charming young widow I met on the train.

The widow and I side by side sat together,
The carriage containing ourselves and no more;
When the silence was broken by my fair companion,
Who enquired the time by the watch that I wore.
I, of course, satisfied her, and then conversation
Was freely indulged in by both, till my brain
Fairly reeled with excitement, I grew so enchanted
With the charming young widow I met on the train.

We became so familiar I ventured to ask
How old was the child she held at her breast.
"Ah, sir," she responded, and into tears bursting,
Her infant, still closer, convulsively pressed.

"When I think of my child, I am well nigh distracted,
Its father, my husband, my heart breaks with pain."
She, choking with sobs, laid her head on my waistcoat,
Did the charming young widow I met on the train.

By this time the train arrived at a station
Within a few miles of the great one in town.
When my charmer exclaimed, as she looked through the window:
"Good gracious alive! Why there goes Mr. Brown.
He's my late husband's brother—dear sir, would you kindly
My best-beloved child for a moment sustain?"
Of course I complied, then off to the platform
Tripped the charming young widow I met on the train.

Three minutes elapsed, when the whistle it sounded,
The train began moving; no widow appeared.
I bawled out, "Stop! Stop!" But they paid no attention.
With a snort and a jerk starting off as I feared.
In this horrid dilemma I sought for the hour.
But my watch—oh, where was it? And where was my chain?
My purse, too, my ticket, my gold pencil case? All gone!
Oh, that artful young widow I met on the train.

While I was my loss so deeply bewailing
The train again stopped and I "Tickets, please," heard.
So I told the conductor, while dandling the infant,
The loss I'd sustained, but he doubted my word.
He called more officials, a lot gathered 'round me,
Uncovered the child—oh, how shall I explain?
For behold, 'twas no baby, 'twas only a dummy.
Oh, the crafty young widow I met on the train!

Satisfied I'd been robbed, they allowed my departure,
Though, of course, I'd settle my fare the next day;
And now I wish to counsel young men from the country
Lest they should get served in a similar way.

Beware of young widows you meet on the railway,
Who lean on your shoulder, whose tears fall like rain;
Look out for your pocket—in case they resemble
The charming young widow I met on the train.

Hop Head

As sung by Judith Tobey

Hop Head went for a dreamy stroll,
   Looking for a pill that he couldn't roll.
Roasted and toasted the whole night through,
   Till he dangled at the end of a chink's bamboo.

Dreamt he had a million nickels and dimes,
   Counted 'em over a million times.
Million girls so pretty and fair,
   With big blue eyes and golden hair.

Went to England to get away from jails,
   There he got acquainted with the Prince of Wales.
Took his watch and his diamond pin—
   And along came a Bobby and run him in.

Went to China for to fight Japan,
   There he got acquainted with Li Hung Chan,
Li Hung Chan said, "Perhaps—
   You'd be better off in Brooklyn shootin' craps."

So he laid his head on a Suey Pow,
And stabbed himself with a Yen Shi Gow,
And in the morning won't you let me in,
   'Cause Hop Sing Toy you're a friend of mine.

Salvation Army Song

As sung by Helen Ramsey

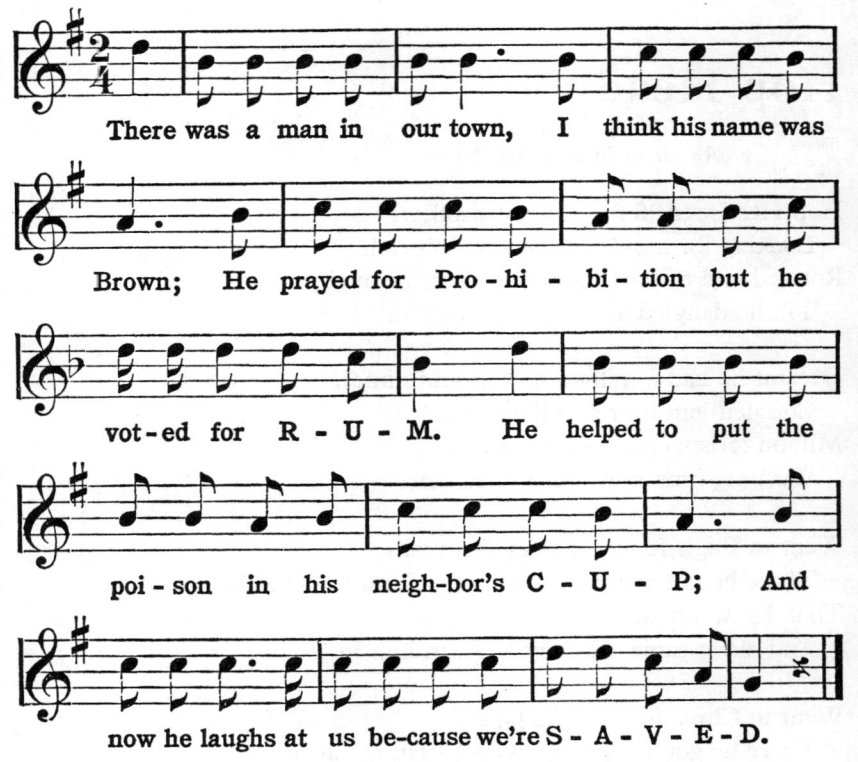

There was a man in our town, I think his name was Brown; He prayed for Pro-hi-bi-tion but he vot-ed for R - U - M. He helped to put the poi-son in his neigh-bor's C - U - P; And now he laughs at us be-cause we're S - A - V - E - D.

Chorus:

Oh G-L-O-R-Y, we are S-A-V-E-D,
H-A-P-P-Y to be F-R-double EE,
Oh V-I-C-T-O-R-Y from the bonds of S-I-N
Glory, glory, Hallelujah, Tra-la-la, Amen.

Some people go on week days
To D-A-N-C-E
They go to church on Sundays
To show their H-A-T.
Some people daub their faces up
With P-A-I-N-T
And then they laugh at us
Because we're S-A-V-E-D.

Chorus

I love to stand on the corner
With my D-R-U-M, drum
It brings to us the sinner
And the B-U-M, bum, bum
They come to us from hovel
And from D-I-T-C-H
And we march on to Victory
Without H-I-T-C-H.

Hannah

I've got a girl named Hannah,
From Butte, Montana.
The reason I don't love her,
She's dead, gol darn her!

She lived on the
Untrodden hills of Butte.
None cared to love her
And none dared to shoot!

The Cannibal Maiden

As sung by Collins B. Reed

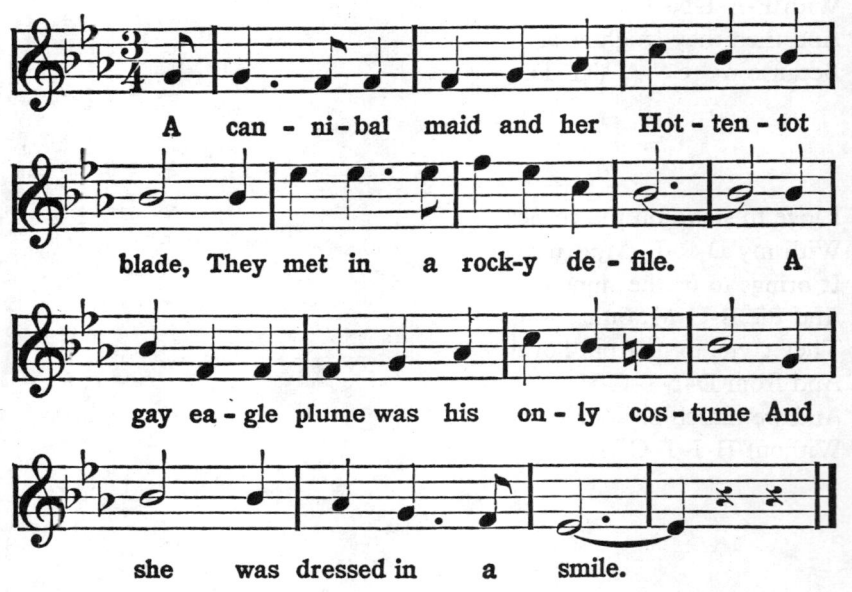

Together they strolled as his passions he told
    In thrilling and tremulous mien,
She had murmured the word when a war whoop was heard,
    And a rival burst out on the scene.

'Twas a savage Zulu to the trysting place drew
    Demanding his cannibal bride,
But the Hottentot said, with a toss of his head,
    "I'll have thy degenerate hide!"

So the Hottentot flew at the savage Zulu
    And the Zulu he flew at the blade;
Together they vied in their strength and their pride
    As they fought for the cannibal maid.

She perched on a stone with her shapely shin bone
    Clasped in her long twining arms,
And watched the blood fly with a love-laden eye
    As the warriors fought for her charms.

Oh, the purple blood flows from the Hottentot's nose,
    And the Zulu is struck by the blade,
As together they vied in their strength and their pride,
    And they died for the cannibal maid.

She made a fine stew of the savage Zulu
    And she scrambled the Hottentot's brains;
'Twas a dainty menu when the cooking was thru
    And she dined from her lovers' remains.

Oh, the savage Zulu and the Hottentot too
    Are asleep in a cannibal tomb;
The three are made one—my story is done,
    And the maiden walked off in the gloom.

Life Is But a Game of Cards

Life is but a game of cards, which each one has to learn:
Each shuffles, cuts and deals a pack, and each a trump does turn:
Some turn a high card at the top, while others turn a low;
Some hold a hand quite full of trumps, while others none can show.

Some shuffle with a practiced hand and pack their cards with care,
So they may know when they are dealt where all the leaders are;
Thus fools are made the dupe of rogue and rogues each other cheat;
But he is very wise, indeed, who never meets defeat.

In playing some will lead the ace, their counting card to save.
Some play the deuce, and some the trey, and many play the knave.
Some play for money, and some for fun, and some for worldly fame.
And not until the game's played out can they count up the gain.

When hearts are trumps some play for love, then pleasure decks the hour.
No thought of sorrow checks our joy in rosy, beauteous bower.
We dance and sing, sweet music make, our cards at random play,
And while the heart remains on top our game is but a holiday.

When diamonds chance to crown the top, then players stake their gold;
And heavy sums are won and lost by gamblers young and old;
Intent on winning, each doth watch his cards with eager eye,
So he may watch his neighbor's hand and cheat him on the sly.

When clubs are trumps, look out for war, on ocean and on land,
For bloody deeds are often done when clubs are in the hand;
Then lives are staked instead of gold, the days are wornout breed,
Across the broad Atlantic now, see clubs have got the lead.

And last of all is when the spade is turned by hand of Time,
And always finishes up the game in every land and clime;
No matter how much a man may win, or how much a man may save,
You'll find the spade turns up at last and digs the player's grave.

Pictures from Life's Other Side

Sung by Hal S. White

Fragment

The next scene was that of a gambler
Who gambled his money away;
Stole a ring from his dead mother's finger
That she wore on her wedding day.
That night he went out on the highway,
"Hands up! Money or your life," he cried.
Then he took with his knife
His own brother's life:
      That's a picture from life's other side!

Old Joe Clark

I don't like Old Joe Clark,
    Don't think I ever shall.
I don't like Old Joe Clark,
    Always liked his girl.

    Rock, rock, rock, Old Joe Clark
        Good-bye, Betsy Brown.
    Rock, rock, rock, Old Joe Clark
        Goin' to leave this town.

Oh, if I had a needle and thread
    As fine as I could sew;
I'd sew myself to Joe Clark's bride
    And down the road we'd go.

    Walk, walk, walk, Old Joe Clark,
        Good-bye, Betsy Brown.
    Walk, walk, walk, Old Joe Clark,
        Say good-bye to your Betsy Brown.

    .   .   .   .   .

John Brown's wife takes whiskey in her tea,
John Brown's wife takes whiskey in her tea,
John Brown's wife takes whiskey in her tea,
    As we go rolling home,

    Glory, glory, hallelujah!
    Glory, glory, hallelujah!
    Glory, glory, hallelujah!
    As we go rolling home.

    .   .   .   .   .

She was an old hen and she had a wooden foot,
    And she made her nest near a huckleberry root;
She laid more eggs than any hen on the farm
    And another little drink wouldn't do us any harm.

Cocaine Bill and Morphine Sue

As sung by Mary Jacobsen

They walked down the East Side full of hope,
Until they saw a sign reading—"No More Dope."

Chorus

Said Bill to Sue, "This will never do,
We gotta get a shot and it's up to you."

Chorus

Sue loved the men and she knew her stuff,
She walked into a drug store prepared to treat 'em rough.

Chorus

She rolled her eyes and she cocked her head
She said, "Come here I want some dope and I won't be misled."

Chorus

She got what she wanted but her tale is sad
Her stuff was good, but the dope was bad.

Chorus

Bill he sighed, and Sue she cried,
And then they both lay down and died.

Chorus

Now in the graveyard side by side
Lie Cocaine Bill and his Morphine bride.

Rollicking Bill the Sailor

This bit must be meat and drink to those initiates who know the correct words. There are many versions, all of them far better than the appended sample, but it is well to remember that the Pilgrims landed on the rock.

"Who's that a-knocking at my door?"
    Cried the fair young maiden.
"Who's that a-knocking at my door?"
    Cried the fair young maiden.

"It's me, myself, and nobody else!"
    Cried Rollicking Bill, the Sailor.
"It's me, myself, and nobody else!"
    Cried Rollicking Bill, the Sailor.

"But we have only one bed!"
    Cried the fair young maiden.
"But we have only one bed!"
    Cried the fair young maiden.

Well, figure it out for yourself and damned be he who first cries, " Hold! Enough!"

Texas Rangers

Come, all you Texas rangers, wherever you may be,
I'll tell you of some troubles that happened unto me.
My name is nothing extra, so it I will not tell,—
And here's to all you rangers, I am sure I wish you well.

It was at the age of sixteen that I joined the jolly band,
We marched from San Antonio down to the Rio Grande.
Our captain he informed us, perhaps he thought it right,
"Before we reach the station, boys, you'll surely have to fight."

And when the bugle sounded our captain gave command,
"To arms, to arms," he shouted, "and by your horses stand."
I saw the smoke ascending, it seemed to reach the sky;
The first thought that struck me, my time had come to die.

I saw the Indians coming, I heard them give the yell;
My feelings at that moment, no tongue can ever tell.
I saw the glittering lances, their arrows round me flew,
And all my strength it left me and all my courage too.

We fought full nine hours before the strife was o'er,
The like of dead and wounded I never saw before.
And when the sun was rising and the Indians they had fled,
We loaded up our rifles and counted up our dead.

All of us were wounded, our noble captain slain,
And the sun was shining sadly across the bloody plain.
Sixteen as brave rangers as ever roamed the West
Were buried by their comrades with arrows in their breast.

'Twas then I thought of mother, who to me in tears did say,
"To you they are all strangers, with me you had better stay."
I thought that she was childish, the best she did not know;
My mind was fixed on ranging and I was bound to go.

Perhaps you have a mother, likewise a sister too,
And maybe you have a sweetheart to weep and mourn for you;
If that be your situation, although you'd like to roam,
I'll advise you by experience, you had better stay at home.

I have seen the fruits of rambling, I know its hardships well;
I have crossed the Rocky Mountains, rode down the streets of hell;
I have been in the great southwest where the wild Apaches roam,
And I tell you from experience you had better stay at home.

And now my song is ended; I guess I have sung enough;
The life of a ranger I am sure is very tough.
And here's to all you ladies, I am sure I wish you well,
I am bound to go a-ranging, so ladies, fare you well.

Cocaine Lil and Morphine Sue

Did you ever hear about Cocaine Lil?
She lived in Cocaine town on Cocaine hill,
She had a cocaine dog and a cocaine cat,
They fought all night with a cocaine rat.

She had cocaine hair on her cocaine head.
She had a cocaine dress that was poppy red;
She wore a snowbird hat and sleigh-riding clothes.
On her coat she wore a crimson, cocaine rose.

Big gold chariots on the Milky Way,
Snakes and elephants silver and gray.
Oh the cocaine blues they make me sad,
Oh the cocaine blues make me feel bad.

Lil went to a snow party one cold night,
And the way she sniffed was sure a fright.
There was Hophead Mag with Dopey Slim
Kankakee Liz and Yen Shee Jim.

There was Morphine Sue and the Poppy Face Kid,
Climbed up snow ladders and down they skid;
There was the Stepladder Kit, a good six feet,
And the Sleigh-riding Sister who were hard to beat.

Along in the morning about half past three
They were all lit up like a Christmas tree;
Lil got home and started for bed,
Took another sniff and it knocked her dead.

They laid her out in her cocaine clothes:
She wore a snowbird hat with a crimson rose;
On her headstone you'll find this refrain:
"She died as she lived, sniffing cocaine."

Oh, No, John!

As sung by the Fuller Sisters

On yonder hill there stands a creature,
   Who she is I do not know;
I'll go and court her for her beauty,
   She must answer "Yes" or "No."
Oh, no, John, no, John, no, John, no.

My father was a Spanish captain,
   Went to sea a month ago;
First he kissed me, then he left me,
   Bade me always answer "No!"
Oh, no, John, no, John, no, John, no.

O madam, in your face is beauty,
   On your lips red roses grow;
Will you take me for your lover?
   Madam, answer "Yes" or "No."
Oh, no, John, no, John, no, John, no.

O madam, I will give you jewels,
  I will make you rich and free,
I will give you silken dresses;
  Madam, will you marry me?
Oh, no, John, no, John, no, John, no.

O madam, if you are so cruel,
  And that you do scorn me so,
If I may not be your lover,
  Madam, will you let me go?
Oh, no, John, no, John, no, John, no.

Then I will stay with you forever,
  Since you will not be unkind;
Madam, I have vowed to love you,
  Would you have me change my mind?
Oh, no, John, no, John, no, John, no.

Hark! I hear the trumpets ringing,
  Will you come and be my wife?
Or, dear madam, have you settled
  To live single all your life?
Oh, no, John, no, John, no, John, no.

Duckfoot Sue

  For now I'll sing to you
    Of the girl I love so true;
She's chief engineer of the night shirt line,
    And her name is Duckfoot Sue.
  Her beauty is all she has;
    She's a mouth as big as a crab;
She has an upper lip like the rudder of a ship,
    And I'll tell you she is mad.

Willie the Weeper

Did you ev-er hear tell a-bout Wil-lie the weep-er,

Wil-lie the weep-er was a chim-ney sweep-er,

Had the dope hab-it and had it bad,

Lis-ten while I'll tell you 'bout the dream he had.

He went to a hop house on Sat'day night,
   'Cause he knew the lights would be burning bright.
Then he smoked a dozen pills or more,
   Dreamt he was living on a foreign shore.

Around a lay-out table a couple of hop-fiends lay,
   Come closer and I'll tell you what they had to say,
Tales of money they were going to make
   And faro banks they were goin' to break.

He went to Monte Carlo and he played roulette,
   He couldn't lose a dollar, won every single bet.
Then they told him that the bank was broke,
   He bought eighteen million dollars worth of coke.

This is the tale of Willie the Weeper,
  Willie the Weeper who was a chimney sweeper,
Went to sleep on his hall-room flop,
  Dreamt he had a million dollars worth of hop.

Hop Song

As Reported by Judge Louis B. Hart

Rich people now they don't take a drop,
  They fill themselves up on cocaine or the hop.
Singing: Oh! Oh! Honey! Baby, won't you be mine?
    Have a (sniff) on me!

Walked up Broadway down on Main,
  Tried to dig up a dime to buy some cocaine.
Singing: Oh! Oh! Honey! Baby, won't you be mine?
    Have a (sniff) on me!

Cocaine's for horses and it's not for men,
  Doctor says 'twill kill you, but don't say when.
Singing: Oh! Oh! Honey! Baby, won't you be mine?
    Have a (sniff) on me!

When I die bury me low,
  Bury me deep in a nice bunch of snow.
Singing: Oh! Oh! Honey! Baby, won't you be mine?
    Have a (sniff) on me!

On the (*sniff*) *the gesture of closing a nostril with one finger and tapping the base of the other with another.*

Johnny Sands

As sung by Harry T. Ramsey

Said he, "My dear, I'll drown myself,
The river runs below."
Said she, "Pray do, you silly elf,
I've wished it long ago."
Says he, "Upon the brink I'll stand.
Do you run down the hill
And push me in with all your might."
Says she, "My dear, I will."
Says she, "My dear, I will."

"For fear that I should courage lack
And try to save my life,
Pray tie my hands behind my back."
"I will," replied his wife.
She tied them fast, as you may think,
And when securely done,
"Now stand, dear John, upon the brink,
And I'll prepare to run.
And I'll prepare to run."

Down, down the hill the loving bride
Now came with all her force
To push him in—he stepped aside,
And she went in of course.

Now splashing, dashing like a fish,
"Oh save me, Johnny Sands."
"I can't, my dear, though much I wish,
For you have tied my hands.
For you have tied my hands."

A Little More Cider

As sung by James O'Reilly

Miss Dinah when she goes to church
She looks so neat and gay.
She has to take the dogs along
To keep the boys away.

Chorus :

> A little more cider
> And a little more cider, too;
> A little more cider for Miss Dinah
> And we all like cider, too

Miss Dinah is a coffee pot
Her nose it is the spout;
And every time she turns around
The coffee it pours out.

Chorus

Miss Dinah when she goes to bed,
She turns herself about.
She puts the candle in the bed
And blows herself right out.

Chorus

Miss Dinah is an ugly bird,
She carries an ugly bill:
She lights right down in the middle of the field
And plucks out hill by hill.

Chorus

I went down to Miss Dinah's home,
Miss Dinah was a-grubbing.
She picked up a club and lit into me
And give me a devil of a clubbing.

Lucky Jim

Jim was my friend, till one unhappy day
   The usual cause—a pretty girl—came in our way.
From that day on we seemed to drift apart,
   For each aspired to win her maiden heart;
But, though I tried each art and winning wile,
   'Twas not on me she gave her sweetest smile;
Each day I saw my chances grow more slim,
   Until—to my despair—one day she married him.
       Ah, lucky Jim!
       How I envied him.

Three years passed on—long years they seemed to me—
   And then Jim died, and once more she was free.
Before me rose the bright hopes of the past;
   I wooed, I sued and married her at last.
I've got my way; and, now she is my wife,
   I know just what there is in married life;
And when I think of Jim, though underground,
   Enjoying peace and quiet most profound—
       Ah, lucky Jim!
       How I envy him.

The Boston Burglar

For burglarizing I was taken and I was sent to jail,
My friends tried to bail me out, but it was of no avail.
The judge he read my sentence, the clerk he wrote it down:
"For seven long and dreary years you are going to Jefferson Town."

To see my aged father come a-pleading to the bar,
To see my aged mother a-pulling her gray hair,
Pulling her old gray locks, my lad, and the tears come streaming down;
Said she, "My son, what have you done? You're going to Jefferson Town."

They put me aboard an east-bound train one cold December day,
And every station that I passed I'd hear the people say;
"There goes that Boston burglar, in chains he's bound down,
For a-robbing of a Boston bank he's going to Jefferson Town."

And there's a girl in Boston; I know she loves me well,
And if ever I regain my liberty 'tis with this girl I'll dwell;
And if ever I regain my liberty, bad company I'll shun,
I'll bid adieu to gambling, night-walking and drinking rum.

Come all you merry fellows, a warning take from me,
And never go a-night-walking and shun bad company,
For if you do, you'll surely rue, and you'll be sent like me,
For seven long and weary years to the stone penitentiary.

Fair Fanny Moore

Down in yonder cottage, all forsaken and forlorn,
The work there neglected and the grass overgrown.
Look in and you'll see some red stains upon the floor.
Alas! it is the blood of the fair Fanny Moore.

The first to come a-courting was young Randall the proud;
He offered fair Fanny his wealth and his word.
His gold and his silver all failed to secure
The heart or the hand of the fair Fanny Moore.

Then next came young Henry, of low-line degree;
He won her fond heart, and enraptured was he.
Straightway to the altar he did then secure
The heart and the hand of the fair Fanny Moore.

As Fanny was sitting in her cottage one day,
When business had called her fond husband away,
Young Randall, the traitor burst open the door,
And clasped in his arms the fair Fanny Moore.

O, Fanny, fair Fanny, reflect upon your fate;
Accept of my offer before it is too late,
There's one thing for certain, I am bound to secure
The life or the love of the fair Fanny Moore.

O, spare me; O, spare me, fair Fanny did cry;
O, spare me; O, spare me; I'm not prepared to die.
Go, then, said the traitor, to the land of the rest,
And he buried his knife in her snowy white breast.

Fair Fanny, all blooming in blood stain, she died;
Young Randall was taken, found guilty and tried;
Young Randall was hanged on a tree by the door,
For shedding the blood of the fair Fanny Moore.

Young Henry, the shepherd, went distracted and wild;
He wandered away from his own native stile;
He wandered away from his own native shore,
Lamenting the fate of the fair Fanny Moore.

He roamed through old Ireland, he roamed through old Spain,
He roamed through old England, returning home again.
At last he was taken from his own cottage door.
And laid in the grave with the fair Fanny Moore.

I've Only Been Down to the Club

As sung by James O'Reilly

Last night I was out rather late;
It was only an innocent spree.
My wife for my coming did wait
When sleeping I thought she would be.
My boots I left down in the hall
And softly I crept up the stair:
I kept rather close to the wall,
And thought to ascend unaware.
But just as I got to the door,
I seemed to get lost in the dark;
I stumbled and fell to the floor,
Just then I could only remark:

Chorus:

The club had a meeting tonight, love,
Of business we had a great sight, love,
Don't think for a moment I'm tight,
I've only been down to the club.

166 *Springfield Mountain*

I found her in temper and tears,
She cried it's a sin and a shame.
She scratched both my eyes and ears,
Just then I could only explain:
She sobbed, she wept and she screamed,
She said she'd go back to her Ma;
While I on the mantel-piece leaned
And tried to enjoy my cigar.
I told her I'd buy her a dress,
If she'd leave me alone for a while;
I gave her a sweet little kiss
When I saw her beginning to smile.

Chorus

Springfield Mountain

On Spring-field Mount-in there did dwell A like-ly youth who was known full well-el - el - el Ri - tu - ri - nu - ri - na.

One Monday morning he did go,
   Out to the meadow for to mow.
         Ri tu ri nu ri na.

A round or two and he did feel,
   When a pizen serpent bit his heel
         Ri tu ri nu ri na.

When he received this deadly wound,
   He dropped his scythe upon the ground.
        Ri tu ri nu ri na.

They carried him to his Polly dear,
   Which made her feel so terribly queer.
        Ri tu ri nu ri na.

And there they put him down to rest,
   And there the poor man slept his last.
        Ri tu ri nu ri na.

The tenth of August in Seventy-one,
   Was when this fateful accident was done.
        Ri tu ri nu ri na.

Let this be a warning to you all,
   To be prepared when your time does call.
        Ri tu ri nu ri na.

My Cottage by the Sea

As sung by D'Arcy Dahlberg

In my cottage by the seashore
   I can see my mountain home:
I can see the hills and valleys
   Where with pleasure I would roam.

All alone, all alone, my love has left me,
   And no other's bride I'll be,
For in my bridal robes he left me
   In my cottage by the sea.

The Hell-bound Train

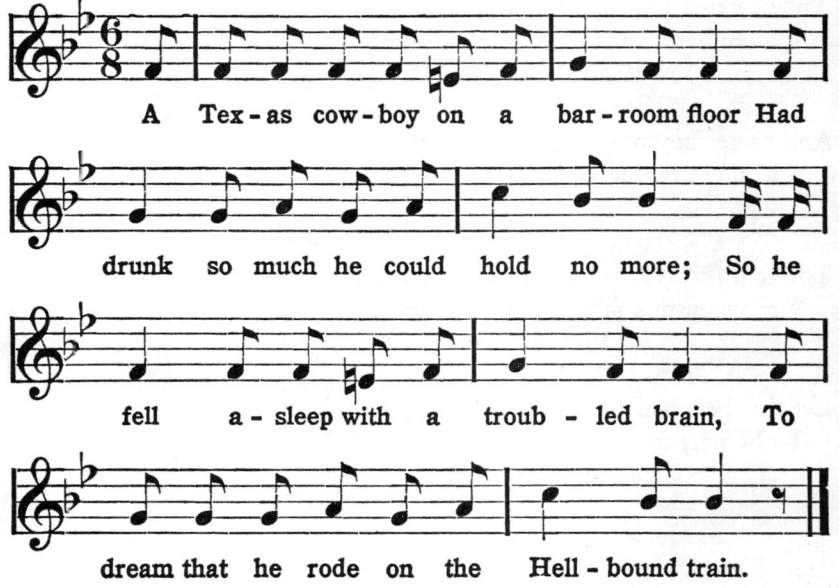

The engine with murderous blood was damp
And was brilliantly lit with a brimstone lamp;
An imp, for fuel, was shoveling bones,
While the furnace rang with a thousand groans.

The boiler was filled with lager beer
And the devil himself was the engineer;
The passengers were a most motley crew,—
Church member, atheist, Gentile, and Jew.

Rich men in broadcloth, beggars in rags,
Handsome young ladies, and withered old hags,
Yellow and black men, red, brown and white,
All chained together—O God, what a sight!

While the train rushed on at an awful pace,
The sulphurous fumes scorched their hands and face;
Wider and wider the country grew,
And faster and faster the engine flew.

Louder and louder the thunder crashed
And brighter and brighter the lightning flashed;
Hotter and hotter the air became
Till the clothes were burnt from each quivering frame.

And out of the distance there arose a yell,
"Ha, ha," said the devil, "we're nearing hell!"
Then oh, how the passengers all shrieked with pain
And begged the devil to stop the train.

But he capered about and danced with glee
And laughed and joked at their misery.
"My faithful friends, you have done your work
And the devil never can pay-day shirk.

"You've bullied the weak, you've robbed the poor;
The starving brother you've turned from the door,
You've laid up gold where the canker rust,
And have given free vent to your beastly lust.

"You've justice scorned, and corruption sown,
And trampled the laws of nature down.
You have drunk, rioted, cheated, plundered and lied,
And mocked at God in your hell-born pride.

"You have paid full fare so I'll carry you through;
For it's only right you should have your due.
Why, the laborer always expects his hire,
So I'll land you safe in the lake of fire.

"Where your flesh will waste in the flames that roar,
And my imps torment you forevermore."
Then the cowboy awoke with an anguished cry,
His clothes wet with sweat and his hair standing high.

Then he prayed as he never had prayed till that hour
To be saved from his sin and the demon's power.
And his prayers and his vows were not in vain;
For he never rode the hell-bound train.

Drunkard John

You might have lit a lamp upon,
   The fiery nose of Drunkard John.
He drank so deep at Backus' bar,
   His breath for miles 'round perfumed the air.

At length his visits long protracted,
   Hath well nigh set his wife distracted,
And fiery embers dimly burned
   Before the boozy sot returned.

At length with patience quite exhausted,
   Her cruel spouse she thus accosted:
"This night you've stayed till after 'leven,
   I wish your soul were safe in heaven.

"I'd rather live in some dark cavern,
   Than see you rolling home from tavern.
If you again return so late,
   To lodge outside must be your fate."

"What, lock me out? You dare not do it,
   For if you do you'll sadly rue it;
I'll drown me in the well hard by,
   And vainly then you'll sob and sigh."

The wife replied, "My mind's at rest,
   I'm sure, dear John, you only jest."
As days rolled on the cruel fetter,
   So galled poor John he walked no better.

But heedless of his gentle wife,
  In wild excitement spent his life.
The sky now dark with many a cloud
  Had clothed the earth in evening shroud.

The moon from view was darkly hidden,
  The stars to shine were all forbidden,
When the good wife in neat attire
  Was sitting by her evening fire.

Sometimes she mused on days gone by;
  Sometimes on some misfortune nigh,
When woke the kettle from its dream
  And from the rising cloud of steam,

A song of mingled woe was heard,
  Unlike the lay of man or bird,
But when the fearful dream was gone,
  Her thoughts were fiercely fixed on John.

"He's not returned, though late the hour
  And though the heavens darkly lower
No entrance to his home he'll find,
  My plan is laid fixed in my mind."

Behold her cover up the fire,
  And softly soon to bed retire.
Refreshing sleep had scarce stole o'er
  The lady's mind when at the door

Came thumps and oaths, a horrid din,
  "Get up and let your husband in."
"Go where you may," the good wife said,
  And as she spoke her husband fled.

Crying, "You'll hear my funeral knell."
  And soon a fearful weight there fell,
And sounds of dashing water come,
  Then all was silent as a tomb.

Drunkard John

"Poor John is drowned. Good Heavens," she cries,
    And rushing from the room she flies,
And hastens to a neighbor near,
    Her mind o'erwhelmed with grief and fear.

Cries "Fire" and "Murder" in one breath,
    "Rise up and rescue John from death.
My husband's drowning in the well,
    I heard the good man when he fell."

Her friends and sons in nature's dress,
    Ran to the place of deep distress.
All in the haste one's knee was hurt,
    When he stumbled and fell and tore his shirt.

Another bruised his tender foot at every pace,
    Till at length they reached the fatal place.
With poles and hooks the well to explore,
    They searched the bottom o'er and o'er.

But did they find the human trunk?
    No, nothing but the bucket sunk.
At last while passing through the door,
    They heard old John with laughter roar.

Who when his good wife fled with haste,
    Himself behind the well-curb placed,
Enjoyed her fright—so cruel hearted—
    And entering in as she departed,

Was safely lying in the bed,
    To hear whate'er was done or said,
And choking and giggling fit to die,
    Could not decide to laugh or cry.

I need not add though oft again,
    Poor John returned with dizzy brain,
And tarried till the latest hour,
    He never found a bolted door.

Once I Loved a Railroad Brakeman

As sung by James O'Reilly

Once I loved a railroad brakeman,
All his thoughts they were of me;
Until a dark-haired girl persuaded him
So now he cares no more for me.

> *Chorus:*
> So go and leave me if you wish to,
> Never let me cross your mind;
> For in this world you love another
> And to her be true and kind.

Many a night with him I rambled,
Many a night with him I spent,
I thought his heart was mine forever,
But I see it was only lent.

> *Chorus*

Many a night he lay sleeping,
Dreaming of love's sweet repose;
While I poor girl lay broken hearted
Listening to the wind that blows.

> *Chorus*

So farewell friends and kind relations,
Farewell to this false young man.
It was he who caused my mind to wander,
Left to mourn the best I can.

Ballad of a Young Man

As sung by Helen Ramsey

And after Work was done
they lured him into a Saloon
and tempted him to drink
a glass of Beer.

But he'd promised his dear old Mother
that he never would Imbibe,
that he'd never touch his Lips to a glass
containing Liquor.

They laughed at him and Jeered
and they called him a cow-yard
Till at last he clutched and drained
the glass of Beer.

When he seen what he had Did
he dashed his glass upon the floor
and Staggered out the door
with Delirium Tremens.

And the first person that he met
was a Salvation Army Lass
and with one kick he broke
her Tambourine.

When she seen what he had Did
She placed a Mark upon his Brow
with a kick that she had learned before
she was Saved.

And the Moral of this tale
is to Shun that Fatal glass
and don't go around kicking
Other people's Tambourines.

The Dog-Catcher's Child

As sung by Helen Ramsey

Je Donnerais Versailles

Je donnerais Versailles
Pour avoir mon ami
La Tour de Notre Dame
La Cloche de mon pays
Et ma jolie colombe
Qui chantait jour et nuit
Auprès de ma blonde
Qu'il fait bon—fait bon—fait bon
Auprès de ma blonde
Qu'il fait bon
Dormir——

The Sailor's Return

Home came the sailor, home from the sea,
And there in the stable a strange horse did see.
"O wife, now tell me what can this mean,
A strange brown horse where my mare should have been?"

 "You old fool, you danged fool, you son-of-a-gun," said she,
 "It's nothing but a milk cow my mother sent to me."
 "Miles have I sailed, five thousand or more,
 But a cow without an udder I never saw before."

Home came the sailor, home from the sea,
And there in the parlor a strange coat saw he.
"O wife, now tell me what can this mean,
A coat that's not mine where my coat should have been?"

 "You old fool, you danged fool, you son-of-a-gun," said she,
 "It's nothing but a blanket my mother sent to me."
 "Miles have I sailed, five thousand or more,
 But buttons on a blanket I never saw before."

Home came the sailor, home from the sea,
And there in his bed a strange face did see.
"O wife, now tell me what does this mean,
Another man's head where my own should have been?"

 "You old fool, you danged fool, you son-of-a-gun," said she,
 "It's nothing but a cabbage head my mother sent to me,"
 "Miles have I sailed, five thousand or more,
 But whiskers on a cabbage head I never saw before."

 Note: The above is the sterilization of a ribald old ballad "Our Gude-Man" page 124, that still finds great favor among men without women. Mr. Charles J. Finger, in his "Frontier Ballads" has another version that many, like this editor, may consider far superior.

The Caissons Are Rolling Along

Artillery Song

Over hill and dale we have hit the dusty trail,
   And those caissons go rolling along.
Countermarch! Right about! Hear those wagon soldiers shout,
   While those caissons go rolling along.

    Chorus:

   Oh, it's hi-hi-yee! For the field artillery,
     Shout out your numbers loud and strong.
   And where'er we go, you will always know
     That the caissons are rolling along,
      That those caissons are rolling along.

To the front, day and night, where the doughboys dig and fight,
   And those caissons go rolling along.
Our barrage will be there, fired on the rocket's red flare,
   While those caissons go rolling along.

    Chorus

With the cavalry boot to boot, we will keep up the pursuit,
   And those caissons go rolling along.
To the front, day and night, where the doughboys dig and fight,
   While those caissons come rolling along.

    Chorus

Young Monroe at Gerry's Rock

A Shanty Boy's Song

It was on a Sunday morning, as you will quickly hear,
   Our logs were piled mountain high, we could not keep them clear.
Our foreman said, "Come, cheer up lads, with hearts relieved of fear,
   We'll break the jam on Gerry's Rock and for Saginaw we'll steer."

Now some of them were willing, while others they were not,
   For to work on jams on Sunday they did not think we ought;
But six of our Canuck boys did volunteer to go
   And break the jam on Gerry's Rock, with a foreman named Monroe.

They had not rolled off many logs when they heard his clear voice say:
   "I'd have you lads on your guard, for the jam will soon give way."
These words were hardly spoken when the mass did break and go,
   And it carried off those six brave lads, and their foreman, Young Monroe.

When the rest of our brave shanty boys, the sad news came to hear,
   In search of their dead comrades, to the river they did steer.
Some of the mangled bodies a-floating down did go,
   While crushed and bleeding near the bank was that of Young Monroe.

They took him from his watery grave, smoothed back his raven hair;
   There was one fair girl among them whose sad cries rent the air;
There was one fair form among them, a maid from Saginaw town,
   Whose moans and cries rose to the skies, for her true lover, who'd gone down.

For Clara was a nice young girl, the riverman's true friend;
   She with her widowed mother dear, lived near the river's bend.
The wages of her own true love the boss to her did pay,
   And the shanty boys for her made up a generous purse next day.

They buried him with sorrow deep, 'twas on the first of May;
   Come all you brave shanty boys and for your comrade pray.
Engraved upon a hemlock tree that by the grave did grow
   Was the name and date of the sad fate of the foreman, Young Monroe.

Fair Clara did not long survive; her heart broke with her grief,
   And scarcely two months later death came to her relief.
And when this time had passed away and she was called to go,
   Her last request was granted, to rest beside Young Monroe.

Come all you brave shanty boys: I would have you call and see
   Those two green mounds by the riverside, where grows the hemlock tree.
The shanty boys cleared off the wood, by the lovers there laid low:
   'Twas the handsome Clara Vernon and our foreman, Young Monroe.

The Midnight Express

As sung by James O'Reilly

"Jim Blake your wife is dying!"
Came over the wires tonight:
The news was brought to the depot
By a lad nigh dead with fright.

He entered the office crying,
His face was awfully white:
"Send this to Dad on his engine,
Mother is dying tonight."

Jim Blake is our oldest driver,
He's running the midnight express:
He's pulled the throttle and lever
For most of his life I guess.

And when I saw the message
Was for my comrade Jim;
You bet I sent it in a hurry,
This sad dispatch to him.

In something less than an hour
Jim's answer came back for her.
"Tell wife I'll be there at midnight;
Tell her I am praying for her."

I left my son in the office,
Took the message to Jim's wife.
There I found a dying woman
With scarcely a breath of life.

When first I entered the chamber,
She took me at first for Jim;
She sank back nigh exhausted
When she saw it was not him.

She raised her eyes to heaven,
Her face was awful white;
She said in a dying whisper,
"God speed the express tonight."

O'er hills and dale and valley,
There thundered the midnight train.
All lighting and sobbing and throbbing
Amid the fearful strain.

But Jim hangs on to the lever,
A-guarding its crazy flight:
While a voice cried out in the darkness,
"God speed the express tonight."

In something less than an hour,
The express will be along.
And here is another message:—
"My God! There is something wrong."

Yes, here it says disaster,
The train is in a ditch.
The engineer is dying,
Derailed by an open switch.

And here is another message,
From the engineer, I guess.
"Tell wife I'll meet her in heaven,
Don't wait for the midnight express."

Bible Stories

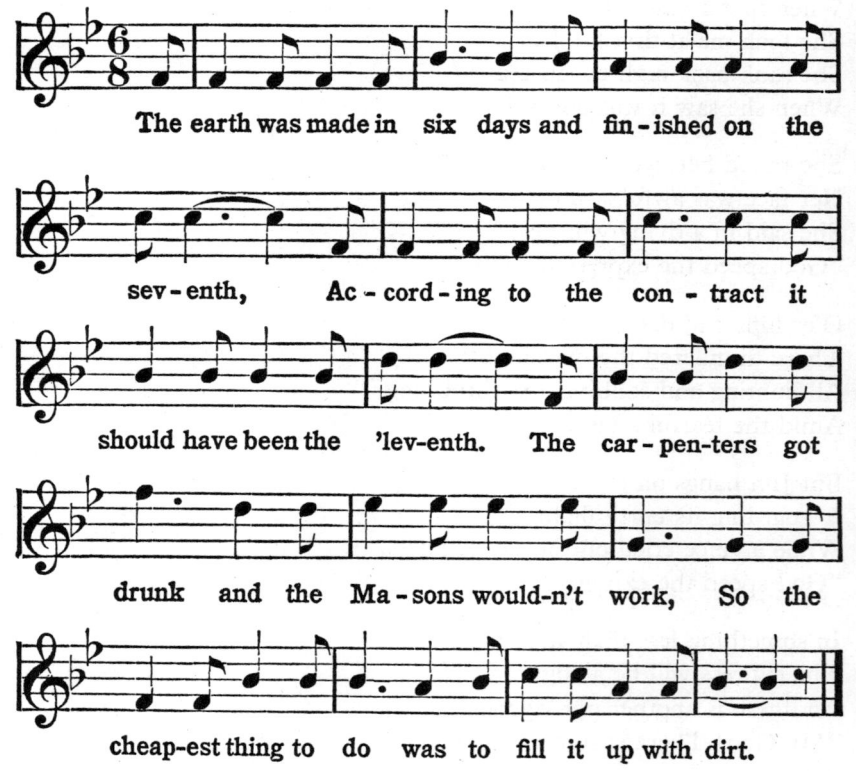

Chorus:
Old folks, young folks, everybody come,
Join the darkies' Sunday school and make yourselves at home.
Kindly check your chewing gum and razors at the door,
And we'll tell you Bible stories that you never heard before.

Adam was the first man and Eve she was his spouse;
They lost their job for stealing fruit and went to keeping house.
All was very peaceful and quiet on the main
Until a little baby came and they started raising Cain.

Chorus

The Lord made the devil, and the devil made sin;
The Lord made a cubbyhole to put the devil in.
The devil got sore and said he wouldn't stay;
The Lord said he had to, 'cause he couldn't get away.

Chorus

Cain he raised potatoes and he peddled them in town.
Abel called him hayseed every time he came around.
Cain he laid a stick of wood on brother Abel's head,
And when he took that stick away, he found poor Abel dead.

Chorus

Noah was the keeper of the Asiatic zoo;
He built an ocean liner when he hadn't much to do;
One day he got excited when the sky was getting dark,
So he gathered all his animals and put them in the ark.

Chorus

It rained for forty days and it rained for forty nights,
The water washed the land completely out of sight!
But when Noah was a-wondering as to what he'd better do
The ark hit Mount Ararat and stuck as tight as glue!

Chorus

Methuselah is famous, because he couldn't croak,
Although he finally grew to be an old and seedy bloke.
He had so many whiskers that you couldn't see his head;
If he'd lived a little longer, he'd have used them for his bed.

Chorus

Bible Stories

Elijah was an aeronaut, or else I am a liar,
He ascended up to heaven in a chariot of fire;
His eccentric disappearance gave the Israelites a shock,
They said he beat the Wright brothers by fully half a block.

Chorus

Abraham was a patriarch, the father of his set;
He took his little Ikey out to kill him on a bet.
And he'd have met his finish if it wasn't for a lamb,
For papa had his razor out and didn't give a damn!

Chorus

Esau was a cowboy of a wild and wooly make,
His father gave him half the land and half to brother Jake;
But when he saw his title to the land it wasn't clear—
He sold it to his brother for a sandwich and a glass of beer!

Chorus

Daniel was a brave man who wouldn't mind the king;
The king he said he never heard of such a thing;
Thrust him down a man-hole with lions all beneath,
But Daniel was a dentist—and pulled the lion's teeth!

Chorus

Jonah was an emigrant, so runs the Bible tale,
He took an ocean voyage in a transatlantic whale.
The whale was over-crowded which put Jonah to distress,
So Jonah pushed the button and the whale did all the rest.

Chorus

David was a shepherd's boy, his mother's pride and joy;
His father gave him a slingshot, a harmless little toy.
Along came Goliath, a-looking for a fuss,
David heaved a cobblestone and caved in his crust.

Chorus

Samson was a strong man of the John L. Sullivan school;
He killed a thousand Philistines with the jawbone of a mule!
Along came a woman who filled him up with gin,
And shaved off his whiskers and the coppers pulled him in.

Final Chorus:

Walk in, walk in, walk in, I say,
Walk into the parlor and hear the banjos play,
Walk into the parlor and hear the banjos ring,
And see the nigger's finger a-picking on the string.

When You and I Were Young, Maggie

When You and I Were Young, Maggie

A city so silent and lone, Maggie,
    Where the young and the gay and the best,
In polished white mansions of stone, Maggie,
    Have each found a place of rest,
Is built where the birds used to play, Maggie,
    And join in the songs that were sung,
For we sang as gay as they, Maggie,
    When you and I were young.

Chorus

They say I am feeble with age, Maggie,
   My steps are less sprightly than then,
My face is a well-written page, Maggie,
   But time alone was the pen.
They say we are aged and gray, Maggie,
   As spray by the white breakers flung;
But to me you're as fair as you were, Maggie,
   When you and I were young.

Chorus

Seven Long Years

A variation of "The Prisoner's Song"

Seven long years I've been married,
Wished that I'd lived an old maid;
For ever since I've been married
My husband won't work at his trade.

He promised me before we were married
That I should be young and gay:
And every night of the week long
Should go to a party or play.

But I have to get up early in the morning,
Toil and toil all the day;
In the evening I have to get supper,
The dishes to wash and put away.

I go to the barroom to find him,
Bring him home if I can.
Young girls you'll never see trouble,
Until you are tied to a man.

But if I'd minded my mother
I'd be at home today.
But being so young and so foolish
The boys have led me astray.

Sometimes I live in the country,
Sometimes I live in the town;
Sometimes I have a great notion
To go to the river and drown.

I wish I had someone to love me,
Someone to call me his own;
Someone to stay with me always,
I'm tired of living alone.

If I had the wings of an angel,
More like the wings of a dove;
I'd fly far over the ocean
And rest in the arms of love.

The Letter Edged in Black

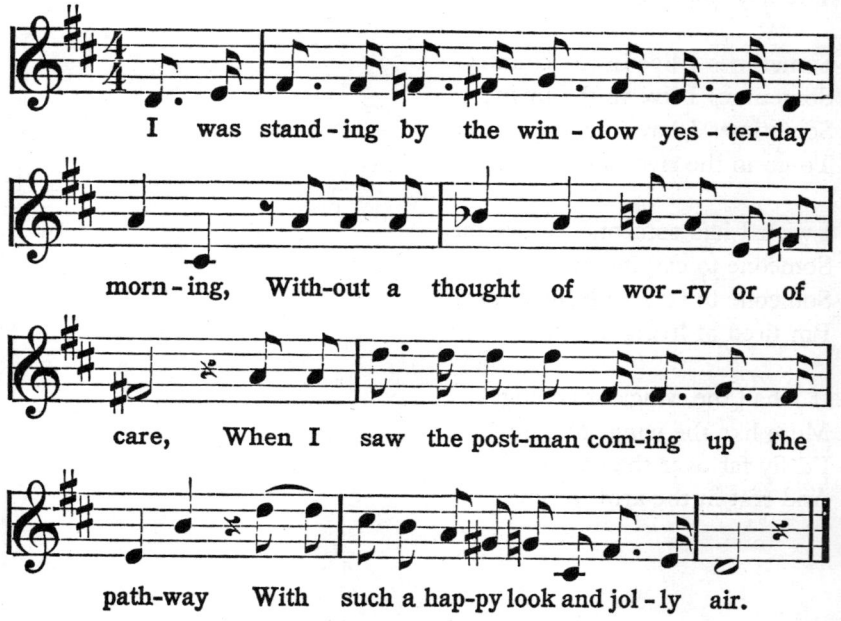

Oh, he rang the bell and whistled while he waited,
And then he said, "Good morning to you, Jack."
But he little knew the sorrow that he brought me
When he handed me a letter edged with black.

   As I heard the postman whistling yester morning,
   Coming down the pathway with his pack,
   Oh, he little knew the sorrow that he brought me
   When he handed me that letter edged in black.

With trembling hand I took the letter from him,
I broke the seal and this is what it said:
"Come home, my boy, your dear old father wants you!
Come home, my boy, your dear old mother's dead!"

The Letter Edged in Black

I could hear the postman whistling yester morning,
Coming down the pathway with his pack,
But he little knew the sorrow that he brought me
When he handed me that letter edged in black.

"The last words that your mother ever uttered—
'Tell my boy I want him to come back,'
My eyes are blurred, my poor old heart is breaking,
For I'm writing you this letter edged in black."

    I could hear the postman whistling yester morning,
    Coming down the pathway with his pack,
    But he little knew the sorrow that he brought me
    When he handed me that letter edged in black.

I bow my head in sorrow and in silence,
The sunshine of my life it all has fled,
Since the postman brought that letter yester morning
Saying, "Come home, my boy, your poor old mother's dead!"

    I could hear the postman whistling yester morning,
    Coming down the pathway with his pack,
    But he little knew the sorrow that he brought me
    When he handed me that letter edged in black.

"Those angry words, I wish I'd never spoken,
You know I never meant them, don't you, Jack?
May the angels bear me witness, I am asking
Your forgiveness in this letter edged in black."

    I could hear the postman whistling yester morning,
    Coming down the pathway with his pack,
    But he little knew the sorrow that he brought me
    When he handed me that letter edged in black.

I'll Give My Love a Cherry

(*Southern Mountain Ballad*)

As sung by Margaret Marshall

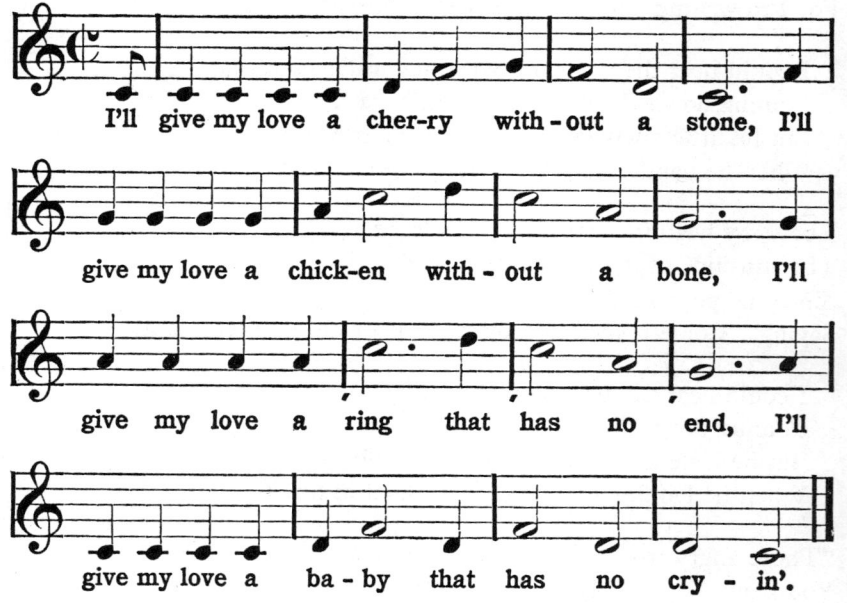

How can there be a cherry without a stone?
How can there be a chicken without a bone?
How can there be a ring that has no end?
How can there be a baby that has no cryin'?

A cherry in the bloom, it has no stone,
A chicken in the egg, it has no bone,
A ring that's rolling, it has no end,
A baby when it's sleepin', it has no cryin'.

Jim Fisk, Jr.

196 Jim Fisk, Jr.

Let me speak of a great man who is now in the grave,
  As good a man as ever was born.
Jim Fisk he was called and his money he gave
  To the outcast, the poor and forlorn.
We all know that he loved both women and wine,
  But his heart it was right, I am sure;
He lived like a prince in his palace so fine,
  But he never went back on the poor.

Jim Fisk was a man, wore his heart on his sleeve,
    No matter what people would say:
He did all his deeds, both the good and the bad,
    In the broad open light of the day:
With his grand six-in-hand at the beach at Long Branch,
    He cut a big dash, to be sure.
But Chicago's big fire showed the world that Jim Fisk
    With his wealth still remembered the poor.

When the telegram came that the poor and distressed
    Were starving to death, slow but sure,
By the lightning express, sent by noble Jim Fisk,
    Went food for the hungry and poor.
Now what do you think of the trial of Stokes,
    Who murdered this friend of the poor?
If such men go free, is any one safe
    To step from outside their own door?

Is there one law for the rich and one for the poor?
    It seems so, at least so they say;
But if they hang up the poor, why hadn't the rich
    Ought to swing up in the very same way?
Don't show any favor to friend or to foe,
    The beggar or prince at your door.
But the millionaire you must hang up also,
    And never go back on the poor.

What's the Use?

As sung by Raymond Hitchcock

Some call this the best old world that nature could contrive,
One thing's sure, that none of us get out of it alive.
Things go on year after year in much the same old style,
Makes you sometimes wonder if anything's worthwhile.
No one knows just where the world is going to so fast,
Life's a great conundrum which we will give up at last.
All the dreaming, all the scheming since the days of yore
Seem to land us just precisely where we were before.
> So what's the use of people growing old and dying if we must be born again?
> O what's the use of all these cunning little babies growing up to homely men?
> O what's the use of lending any one a five-spot if the next time he borrows ten?
> All single folks 'tis said often wish that they were wed
> And those who are wish they were dead.
> > So what's the use?

What's the use of drinking if you always have a thirst?
Twenty drinks will make you far more thirsty than the first.
Seems to me to take a bath is quite a hopeless case!
You'll get dirty once again and wash the same old face!

What's the use of giving good advice to people now?
Wise men need it not and fools don't take it anyhow.
Take the straight and narrow path, the parsons always say.
What's the use of telling that to the people on Broadway.
> So what's the use of fellows having lots of push if some one else has got the pull?
> O what's the use of speculating all your cash, if you're a bear you make a bull?
> O what's the use of people saying you're a bear if then they fleece you for your wool?
> It's the old bull con, you are a lamb and later on you are a lobster when it's gone,
> > So what's the use?

Get Away, Old Man, Get Away!

Now listen all you girls when you go to choose a man,
  Don't take one who is ancient, get a young one if you can.
For an old man he is old, and an old man he is gray,
  But a young man knows just how to love—
    Get away, old man, get away!

Don't ever marry an old man, you'll find it doesn't pay,
  For you'll soon meet a young man, who will steal your heart away.
For an old man, etc.

You want to find a young man with healthy rosy cheeks,
  For if an old man gets the rheumatiz he stays in bed for weeks.
For an old man, etc.

I wouldn't marry an old man, I'll tell you the reason why,
  Tobacco juice is on his lips and his chin is never dry.
For an old man, etc.

I'd rather marry a young man with a goodly supply of brains,
  For there's no fool like an old fool and you cannot make him change.
For an old man, etc.

An old man may have money and cattle for his farm,
  But a young man hugs much better for there is power in his arm.
For an old man, etc.

An old man and a young girl should never, never mix,
  For no one ever found out how to teach an old dog new tricks.
For an old man, etc.

Be sure to marry a young man no matter what the cost,
  For an old man's like an apple when bitten by the frost.
For an old man he is old, and an old man he is gray,
  But a young man knows just how to love—
    Get away, old man, get away!

Dis Mornin', Dis Evenin', So Soon

As Sung by William B. Smith, and nicely, too

Tell old Bill, when he leaves home dis mornin',
Tell old Bill, when he leaves home dis evenin',
Tell old Bill, when he leaves home, To let dem down-town coons a-lone, Dis mornin', dis evenin', so soon.

Bill left home by de alley gate, dis mornin',
Bill left home by de alley gate, dis evenin',
Bill left home by de alley gate,
But he couldn't outrun that thirty-eight!
Dis mornin', dis evenin', so soon.

Old Bill's wife was a-bakin' bread, dis mornin,'
Old Bill's wife was a-bakin' bread, dis evenin',
Old Bill's wife was a-bakin' bread,
When they told her Bill had been shot dead
Dis mornin', dis evenin', so soon.

Oh no, dat can't be so, dis mornin',
Oh no, dat can't be so, dis evenin',
Oh no, dat can't be so:
For Bill lef' home but an hour ago,
Dis mornin', dis evenin', so soon.

Oh no, dat cannot be, dis mornin',
Oh no, dat cannot be, dis evenin',
Oh no, dat cannot be,
For to shoot my husban' in de firs' degree,
Dis mornin', dis evenin', so soon.

Dey brought Bill home wid his toe-nails draggin', dis mornin',
Dey brought Bill home wid his toe-nails draggin', dis evenin',
Dey brought Bill home wid his toe-nails draggin',
Dey was taking Bill home in de hurry-up wagon,
Dis mornin', dis evenin', so soon.

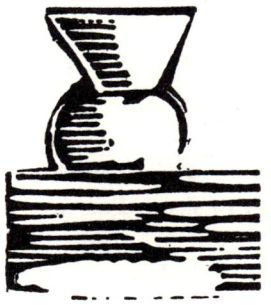

The Dying Ranger

As sung by D'Arcy Dahlberg

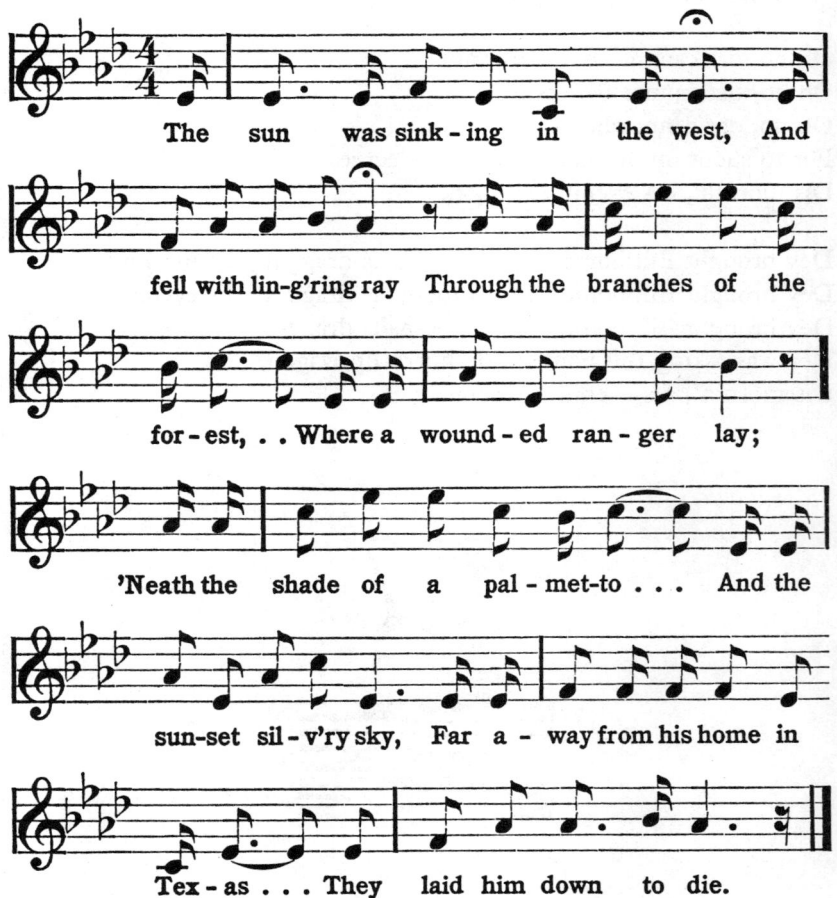

The sun was sinking in the west, And fell with lin-g'ring ray Through the branches of the for-est, .. Where a wound-ed ran-ger lay; 'Neath the shade of a pal-met-to ... And the sun-set sil-v'ry sky, Far a-way from his home in Tex-as ... They laid him down to die.

A group had gathered round him,
His comrades in the fight,
A tear rolled down each man's cheek
As he bid a last good-night.
One tried and true companion
Was kneeling by his side,
To stop his life-blood flowing,
But alas, in vain he tried.

When to stop the life-blood flowing
He found 'twas all in vain,
The tears rolled down each man's cheek
Like light showers of rain.
Up spoke the noble ranger,
"Boys, weep no more for me,
I am crossing the deep waters
To a country that is free

"Draw closer to me, comrades,
And listen to what I say,
I am going to tell a story
While my spirit hastens away.
Way back in Northwest Texas,
That good old Lone Star State,
There is one that for my coming
With a weary heart will wait.

"A fair young girl, my sister,
My only joy, my pride,
She was my friend from boyhood,
I had no one left beside.
I have loved her as a brother,
And with a father's care
I have strove from grief and sorrow
Her gentle heart to spare.

The Dying Ranger

"My mother, she lies sleeping
Beneath the church-yard sod,
And many a day has passed away
Since her spirit fled to God.
My father, he lies sleeping
Beneath the deep blue sea,
I have no other kindred,
There are none but Nell and me.

"But our country was invaded
And they called for volunteers;
She threw her arms around me,
Then burst into tears,
Saying, 'Go, my darling brother,
Drive those traitors from our shore,
My heart may need your presence,
But our country needs you more.'

"It is true I love my country,
For her I gave my all.
If it hadn't been for my sister,
I would be content to fall.
I am dying, comrades, dying,
She will never see me more,
But in vain she'll wait my coming
By our little cabin door.

"Comrades, gather closer
And listen to my dying prayer:
Who will be to her as a brother,
And shield her with a brother's care?"
Up spake the noble rangers,
They answered one and all,
"We will be to her as brothers
Till the last one does fall."

One glad smile of pleasure
O'er the ranger's face was spread;
One dark, convulsive shudder
And the ranger boy was dead.
Far from his darling sister
We laid him down to rest
With his saddle for a pillow
And his gun across his breast.

Shanahan's Ould Shebeen

By Gerald Brennan

This is the tale that Cassidy told
In his halls a-sheen with purple and gold:
  —Told as he sprawled in an easy chair,
  Chewing cigars at a dollar a pair.
  —told with a sigh and perchance a tear
  As the rough soul showed through the cracked veneer;
  —Told as he gazed on the walls near by,
  Where a Greuze and a Millet were hung on high,
  With a rude little print in a frame between—
A picture of Shanahan's old shebeen.

"I'm drinkin' me mornin's mornin'—but it doesn't taste the same;
Though the glass is iv finest crystal, an' the liquor slips down like crame;
An' me cockney footman brings it on a soort of a silver plate,—
Sherry and bitters it is; whiskey is out iv date.
In me bran' new brownstone manshin'—Fift' av'noo over th' way,
Th' Cathedral round th' corner, an' the Lord Archbishop to tay,
Sure I ought to be sthiff with grandeur, but me tastes are mighty mean,
An' I'd rather a mornin's mornin' at Shanahan's ould shebeen.

"Oh! well do I mind th' shanty—th' rocks, an' the field beyant,
The dirt floor yellow wid sawdust, an' th' walls on a three-inch shlant.
There's a twelve-story 'flat' on th' site now—('twas meself that builded the same),

An' they called it 'The Mont-morincy'—though I wanted the good
  ould name.
Me dinner-pail under me oxther, before th' whistle blew,
I'd banish th' drames from me eyelids wid a noggin', or maybe two;
An' oh! 'twas th' illigant whisky—its like I have never seen
Since I went for me mornin's mornin' to Shanahan's ould shebeen.

"I disremember th' makers—I couldn't tell you th' brand;
But it smiled like the golden sunlight, an' it looked an' tasted gr-rand.
When me throat was caked with morthar an' me head was cracked wid
  a blast,
One drink o' Shanahan's dewdrops an' all me troubles was past.
That's why, as I squat on th' cushins, wid divil a hap'orth to do,
In a mornin' coat lined wid velvet, an' a champagne lunch at two,
The' mem'ry comes like a banshee meself an' me wealth between;
An' I long for a mornin's mornin' in Shanahan's ould shebeen.

"A mornin' coat lined wid velvit—an' me ould coat used to do
Alike for mornin' an' evenin' (an' sometimes I slep' in it, too),
An' 'twas divil a sup iv sherry that Shanahan kept—no fear;
If you couldn't afford good whisky, he'd take you on trust for beer.
Th' dacintest gang I knew there—McCarthy (Sinathor since),
An' Murphy that mixed th' morthar (sure th' Pope has made him a
  Prince),
You should see 'em, avic, o' Sundays, wid faces scraped an' clean,
When th' boss stood a mornin's mornin' round Shanahan's ould
  shebeen.

"Whist!—here comes his Grace's carriage; 'twill be lunchtime by an'
  by;
An' I dasn't drink another, though me throat is powerful dry;
For I've got to meet th' Archbishop—I'm a laborer now no more,
—But, ohone! those were fine times, then, lad, an' to talk o' 'em makes
  me sore.
An' whisper—there's times, I tell you, when I'd swap this easy chair,
An' the velvet coat, an' th' footman, wid his Sassenach nose in th' air,
—An th' Lord Archbishop himself, too, for a drink o' th' days that ha'
  been,
For th' taste o' a mornin's mornin' in Shanahan's ould shebeen."

Sally Brown

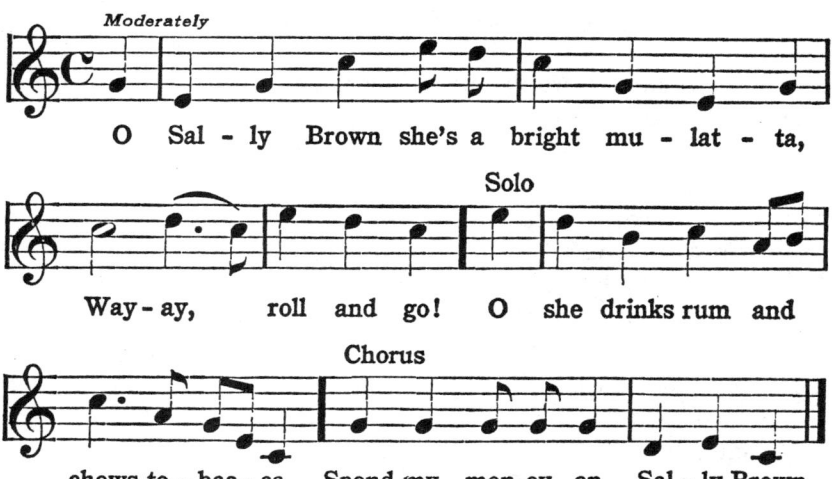

Seven long years I courted Sally.
She said, "O boy, why do you dally?"

Oh Sally Brown, I long to see you!
Oh Sally Brown, I'll not deceive you!

Sally Brown's a creole lady;
I guess she's got a yellow baby.

Oh Sally Brown, what is the matter?
Pretty gal, but can't get at her.

Oh Sally lives on the old plantation,
A member of the creole nation.

Now all my troubles they are over,
   Way-ay, roll and go!

Sally's married to a cullud soldier,
   I'll spend no money on Sally Brown.

The Recruit

By Robert William Chambers

Sez Corporal Madden to Private McFadden:
"Bedad, yer a bad'un!
Now, turn out yer toes
Yer belt is unhookit!
Yer cap is on crookit!
Ye may not be dhrunk,
But, be-jabers, ye look it.
    Wan,—two!
    Wan,—two!
Ye monkey-face divil, I'll jolly ye through!
    Wan,—two!
    Time! Mark!
Ye march like an aigle in Cintheral Park!"

Sez Corporal Madden to Private McFadden:
"A saint it ud sadden
To drill such a mug!
Eyes front! ye baboon, ye.
Ye've jaws like a goat,—
Halt! ye leather-lipped loon, ye!
    Wan,—two!
    Wan,—two!
Ye whiskered ourang-outang, I'll fix you!
    Wan,—two!
    Time! Mark!
Ye've eyes like a bat!
Can ye see in the dark?"

Sez Corporal Madden to Private McFadden:
"Yer figger wants padd'n—
Sure, man, ye've no shape!
Behin' ye, yer shoulders stick out like two bowlders;

Yer shins is as thin
As a pair of pen-holders.
    Wan,—two!
    Wan,—two!
Yer belly belongs on yer back, it do!
    Wan,—two!
    Time! Mark!
I'm as dhry as a dog,—I can't shpake, but I bark!"

Sez Corporal Madden to Private McFadden:
"Me heart it ud gladden
To blacken yer eye,
Yer getting too bold, ye
Compel me to scold ye,—
'Tis 'Halt' that I say—
Will ye heed what I told ye?
    Wan,—two!
    Wan,—two!
Be-jabers I'm dhrier than Brian Boru!
    Wan,—two!
    Time! Mark!
What's wu'ruk for chickens is sport for a lark!"

Sez Corporal Madden to Private McFadden:
"I'll not stay a-gadd'n
With monkeys like you!
I'll travel no farther,
I'm dying for wather;—
Come on, if ye like—
Can ye loan me a quarter!
    Ya-as, you,
    What? two?
And ye'll pay the potheen? Ye're a daisy. Whurroo!
    You'll do!
    Whist! Mark!
The Rigimint's flattered to own ye, me spark!"

The Flying Cloud

The Flying Cloud

My father bound me to a trade in Waterford's fair town,
He bound me to a cooper there, by the name of William Brown.
I served my master faithfully for eighteen months or more,
Then I shipped on board of the Ocean Queen, belonging to Tramore.

When we came unto Bermuda's isle, there I met with Captain Moore,
The commander of the Flying Cloud, hailing from Baltimore;
He asked me if I'd ship with him, on a slaving voyage to go,
To the burning shores of Africa, where the sugar cane does grow.

It was after some week's sailing we arrived on Africa's shore,
And five hundred of those poor slaves, my boys, from their native land we bore
We made them walk in on a plank, and we stowed them down below;
Scarce eighteen inches to a man was all they had to go.

The plague and fever came on board, swept half of them away;
We dragged the bodies up on deck and hove them in the sea.
It was better for the rest of them that they had died before,
Than to work under brutes of planters in Cuba forevermore.

It was after stormy weather we arrived off Cuba's shore,
And we sold them to the planters there to be slaves forevermore.
For the rice and the coffee seed to sow beneath the broiling sun,
There to lead a wretched lonely life till their career was run.

It's now our money is all spent, we must go to sea again,
When Captain Moore he came on deck and said unto us men,
"There is gold and silver to be had with me you'll remain,
And we'll hoist the pirate flag aloft, and we'll scour the Spanish Main."

We all agreed but three young men who told us them to land,
And two of them were Boston boys, the other from Newfoundland.
I wish to God I'd joined those men and went with them on shore,
Than to lead a wild and reckless life, serving under Captain Moore.

The Flying Cloud was a Yankee ship of five hundred tons or more:
She could outsail any clipper ship hailing out of Baltimore.
With her canvas white as the driven snow, and on it there's no specks,
And forty men and fourteen guns she carried on her decks.

It's oft I've seen that gallant ship with the wind abaft her beam,
With her royals and her stunsails set, a sight for to be seen;
With the curling waves at her clipper bow, a sailor's joy to feel,
And the canvas taut in the whistling breeze, logging fourteen off the reel.

We sank and plundered many a ship down on the Spanish Main,
Caused many a wife and orphan in sorrow to remain;
To them we gave no quarter, but gave them watery graves,
For the saying of our captain was that dead men tell no tales.

Pursued we were by many a ship, by frigates and liners too,
Till at last a British man-o'-war, the Dungeness, hove in view,
She fired a shot across our bow, as we sailed before the wind,
Till a chainshot cut our mainmast down, and we fell far behind.

Our crew they beat to quarters as she ranged up along-side,
And soon across our quarter-deck there ran a crimson tide.
We fought till Captain Moore was killed and twenty of our men,
Till a bombshell set our ship on fire, we had to surrender then.

It's next to Newgate we were brought, bound down in iron chains,
For the sinking and the plundering of ships on the Spanish Main.
The judge he found us guilty, we were condemned to die;
Young men, a warning by me take, and shun all piracy.

Then fare you well, old Waterford, and the girl I adore;
I'll never kiss your cheek again, or squeeze your hand no more.
For whiskey and bad company first made a wretch of me;
Young men, a warning by me take, and shun all piracy.

The Girl in the Blue Velvet Band

In that city of wealth, beauty and fashion;
Dear old 'Frisco, where I first saw the light,
And the many frolics that I had there
Are still in my memory tonight.

One evening while out for a ramble;
Here or there without thought or design,
I chanced on a young girl, tall and slender,
At the corner of Kearney and Pine.

On her face was the first flush of nature,
And bright eyes seemed to expand;
While her hair fell in rich, brilliant tresses,
Was entwined in a blue velvet band.

To a house of gentle ruination,
She invited me with a sweet smile;
She seemed so refined, gay and charming
That I thought I would tarry awhile.

She then shared with me a collection
Of wines of an excellent brand,
And conversed in the politest language;
The girl with the blue velvet band.·

After lunch to a well-kept apartment,
We repaired to the third floor above;
And I thought myself truly in heaven,
Where reigneth the Goddess of Love.

Her lady's taste was resplendent,
From the graceful arrangement of things;
From the pictures that stood on the bureau,
To the little bronze Cupid with wings.

But what struck me most was an object
Designed by an artistic hand;
'Twas the costly layout of a hop-fiend,
And the fiend was my blue velvet band.

On a pile of soft robes and pillows
She reclined, I declined on the floor,
Then we both hit the pipe and I slumbered,
I pondered it over and o'er.

'Tis months since the craven arm grasped me,
And in bliss did my life glide away;
From opium to 'dipping' and thieving,
She artfully led day by day.

One evening, coming home wet and weary,
With the swag from a jewelry store;
I heard the soft voice of my loved one,
As I gently opened the door.

"If you'll give me a clue to convict him,"
Said a stranger, in tones soft and bland,
"You'll then prove to me that you love me."
"It's a go," said my blue velvet band.

Ah! How my heart filled with anger,
At woman, so fair, false, and vile,
And to think that I once truly adored her,
Brought to my lips a contemptuous smile.

All ill-gotten gains we had squandered
And my life was hers to command;
Betrayed and deserted for another—
Could this be my blue velvet band?

Just few moments before I was hunted
By the cops, who wounded me, too,
And my temper was none the sweetest,
As I swung myself into their view.

And the copper, not liking the glitter
Of the "44" Colt in my hand,
Hurriedly left through the window,
Leaving me with my blue velvet band.

What happened to me I will tell you:
I was ditched for a desperate crime,
There was hell in a bank about midnight,
And my pal was shot down in his prime.

As a convict of hard reputation,
Ten years of hard grind I did land,
And I often thought of the pleasures
I had with my blue velvet band.

One night as bed time was ringing,
I was standing close to the bars,
I fancied I heard a girl singing,
Far out in the ocean of stars.

Her voice had the same touch of sadness
I knew that but one could command,
I had the same thrill of gladness
As that of my blue velvet band.

Many months have passed since this happened,
And the story belongs to the past;
I forgave her, but just retribution
Claimed this fair but false one at last.

She slowly sank lower and lower,
Down through life's shifting sands,
Till finally she died in a hop joint,
This girl with the blue velvet band.

If she had been true when I met her,
A bright future for us was in store,
For I was an able mechanic,
And honest and square to the core.

216 *The Girl in the Blue Velvet Band*

But as sages of old have contended,
What's decreed we mortals must stand;
So a grave in the Potter's field ended
My romance with the blue velvet band.

Now, when I get out I will hasten
Back to my home town again,
Where my chances are good for some dollars,
All the way from a thousand to ten.

And if I'm in luck I'll endeavor
To live honest in some other land,
And bid farewell to dear old 'Frisco,
And the grave of my blue velvet band.

The Millman Tragedy

By Mrs. C. A. Barron

Lines on the death of William Millman, who was executed at Charlottetown, P. E. I., on April 10, 1888, for the foul murder of Mary Tuplin.

Both old and young, come ponder well, what I shall now relate
Of this most awful tragedy in Charlottetown of late:
The murderer, of whom I write, few years beyond a boy,
William Millman was his name, his mother's hope and joy.

She brought him up so tenderly, and did a mother's part,
Nor dreamed that time so near at hand, when he would break her heart;
Yes, break both parents' hearts—I can't describe the sorrow they must feel,
No matter where on earth they go, their griefs are with them still.

The memory of that much-loved son, his mother's eyes behold.
With murder of the deepest dye on his immortal soul:
To look upon that fine young man, no one would e'er have thought
So horrible a crime as that would enter his young heart.

Against the girl whom he had vowed he never would deceive.
Poor innocent! She could do naught but his false vows believe.
Shame on the base deceiver, whose cruel heart was bent
On taking her poor life away—for that was his intent.

It is of her I now must speak, her cruel death recall.
Her broken-hearted parents dear, the saddest thought of all.
Their hearts were filled with grief, for they were mourning for their son.
And while their tears were falling fast, this dreadful deed was done.

'Twas Mary Tuplin, young and fair—her household duties o'er,
Went forth to meet her lover, as she oft had done before:
And as she tripped along the path, one look at home she cast,
Though in her heart she never dreamed that it would be her last.

Her thoughts were sad, for brother dear—alas! 'twas that same day
She stood beside his silent grave and saw him laid away;
The tears were fresh upon her cheeks as she went on her way,
Anxious to meet with him she loved, to wipe those tears away.

She hoped that he would share her grief, perhaps her thoughts had been
That if his heart were sore depressed, how she would comfort him.
But not a man, a monster, worse, a demon, waited there;
A monster would not raise his hand to one so young and fair.

They met, poor girl, what horrid fate, what anguish did she bear;
Could her poor rigid corpse but speak, alas! what should we hear?
What agonizing cries and prayers to him her life to spare,
As with the weapon in his hand—she sees the pistol near.

Her fair young life he took, and when the last faint spark was gone,
He to the river dragged her then, tied to a heavy stone;
And as he cast her body in, he slyly looked around,
Saying, "No one will ever think of this; she never will be found."

But O, the eye of God was on his every movement there,
And soon before the neighbors He all traces did lay bare;
Her body was discovered soon, beneath the flowing wave,
At the botton of the river he had planned to be her grave.

Her parents laid her in the tomb, close by her brother's side,
Their happiness forever gone, their peace of mind denied;
O, cruel-hearted, false young man, who led that girl astray,
And baser still, to hide his sin, he took her life away.

Now pray, young men, a warning take, from friends who wish you well,
Remember Millman, while he lay, chained in his lonely cell;
Think of his anguish and despair, when told that he must die,
That he must pay the forfeit for the laws that he'd defy.

Think of your parents and of his, their hearts, what grief they know;
They never can look up again in this world of sin and woe;

Think of that young girl, who did on his promise rely,
Whom he sent to meet her Maker—all unprepared to die.

And all young girls who read these lines, before it is too late,
Be cautious in your conduct, lest you meet the same sad fate;
And when in company with men, be prudent and take care,
Put no temptation in their way—of flatterers beware.

They may seem kind and loving words, they whisper in your ear,
But seek advice from those who know, to judge if they're sincere;
And mothers who have children dear, O, every day and hour,
Pray to the God, who rules above, to keep them by His power.

Now ponder well, young people all, and pray this warning take,
Be careful in your friendships and choose a proper mate;
Honor your dear parents, and keep the laws divine,
And happiness and peace will be your portion for all time.

The Closing Scene

From Millman's eyes the streaming tears in bitter anguish fell,
While to his friends and all he knew he bade a last farewell;
Then "Cover up my eyes," he said, "that I may never see
The gallows, or that dreadful rope that now awaiteth me."

Poor Millman paid the penalty—he lies beneath the sod;
We leave him to the tender mercies of a most loving God.

In Bohemia Hall

In Bohemia Hall

Copyright, 1926, by Louis B. Hart, Buffalo, N. Y.

The Actor's Story

By George E. Simmons

Mine is a wild, strange story, the strangest you ever heard;
There are many who won't believe it, but it's gospel, every word;
It's the biggest drama of any in a long, adventurous life;
The scene was a ship, and the actors were myself and my new-wed wife.

You mustn't mind if I ramble and lose the thread now and then;
I'm old, you know, and I wander—it's a way with old women and men.
For their lives all lie behind them, and their thoughts go far away,
And are tempted afield, like children lost on a Summer day.

The years must be five-and-twenty that have passed since that awful night,
But I see it again this evening; I can never shut out the sight.
We were only a few weeks married; I and the wife, you know,
When we had an offer for Melbourne, and made up our minds to go.

We'd acted together in England, traveling up and down
With a strolling band of players, going from town to town;
We played the lovers together—we were leading lady and gent—
And at last we played in earnest and straight to the church we went.

The parson gave us his blessing, and I gave Nellie the ring.
And swore that I'd love and cherish and endow her with everything;
How we smiled at that part of the service, when I said "I thee endow."
But as to the "love and cherish," friend, I meant to keep that vow.

We were only a couple of strollers; we had coin when the show was good.
When it wasn't we went without it, and we did the best we could;
We were happy and loved each other, and laughed at the shifts we made.
Where love makes plenty of sunshine there poverty casts no shade.

Well, at last we got to London, and did pretty well for a bit;
Then the business dropped to nothing and the manager took a fit—

Stepped off one Sunday morning, forgetting the treasury call;
But our luck was in, and we managed right on our feet to fall.

We got an offer for Melbourne—got it that very week.
Those were the days when thousands went over their fortunes to seek—
The days of the great gold fever, and a manager thought the spot
Good for a "spec," and took us actors among his lot.

We hadn't a friend in England—we'd only ourselves to please—
And we jumped at the chance of trying our fortune across the seas.
We went on a sailing vessel, and the journey was long and rough;
We hadn't been out a fortnight before we had had enough.

But use is a second nature, and we'd got not to mind a storm.
When misery came upon us—came in a hideous form.
My poor little wife fell ailing, grew worse, and at last so bad
That the doctor said she was dying—I thought 'twould have sent me mad.

Dying, where leagues of billows seemed to shriek for their prey,
And the nearest land was hundreds—aye, thousands of miles away.
She raved one night in a fever, and the next lay still as death,
So still I'd bend to listen for the faintest sign of breath.

She seemed in a sleep, and sleeping with a smile on her thin, wan face,
She passed away one morning, while I prayed to the throne of grace.
I knelt in the little cabin, and prayer after prayer I said
Till the surgeon came and told me it was useless—my wife was dead!

Dead! I wouldn't believe it. They forced me away that night,
For I raved in my wild despairing, the shock sent me mad outright,
I was shut in the farthest cabin, and I beat my head on the side,
And all day long in my madness, "They've murdered her!" I cried.

They locked me away from my fellows—put me in cruel chains.
It seems I had seized a weapon to beat out the surgeon's brains;
I cried in my wild, mad fury that he was the devil sent
To gloat o'er the frenzied anguish with which my heart was rent.

I spent that night with the irons heavy upon my wrists;
And my wife lay dead quite near me. I beat with my fettered fists,
Beat at my prison panels, and then, O God! and then
I heard the shrieks of women and the tramp of hurrying men.

I heard the cry, "Ship afire!" caught up by a hundred throats,
And over the roar the captain shouting to lower the boats;
Then cry upon cry, and curses, and the crackle of burning wood,
And the place grew hot as a furnace—I could feel it where I stood.

I beat at the door and shouted, but never a sound came back,
And the timbers above me started, till right through a yawning crack
I could see the flames shooting upward, seizing on mast and sail,
Fanned in their burning fury by the breath of the howling gale.

I dashed at the door in fury, shrieking, "I will not die!
Die in this burning prison!"—but I caught no answering cry.
Then, suddenly, right upon me the flames crept up with a roar,
And their fiery tongues shot forward, cracking my prison door.

I was free—with the heavy iron door dragging me down to death,
I fought my way to the cabin, choked with the burning breath
Of the flames that danced around me like mad, mocking fiends at play,
And then—O God! I can see it, and shall to my dying day.

There lay my Nell as they'd left her, dead in her berth that night;
The flames flung a smile on her features—a horrible, lurid light.
God knows how I reached and touched her, but I found myself by her side;
I thought she was living a moment; I forgot that my Nell had died.

In the shock of those awful seconds reason came back to my brain,
I heard a sound as of breathing, and then a low cry of pain.
O, was there mercy in Heaven? Was there a God in the skies?
The dead woman's lips were moving, the dead woman opened her eyes.

I cursed like a madman raving—I cried to her, "Nell, my Nell!"
They had left us alone and helpless, alone in that burning hell;

They had left us alone to perish—forgotten me living—and she
Had been left for the fire to bear her to Heaven, instead of the sea.

I clutched her, roused her, shrieking, the stupor was on her still;
I seized her in spite of my fetters—fear gave me a giant's will.
God knows how I did it, but blindly I fought through the flames and the wreck,
Up, up to the air, and brought her to the deck.

We'd a moment of life together—a moment of life, the time
For one last word to each other—'twas a moment, supreme, sublime.
From the trance we'd for death mistaken the heat had brought her to life,
And I was fettered and helpless—so we lay there, husband and wife!

It was but a moment, but ages seemed to have pased away,
When a shout came over the water, and I looked, and lo, there lay
Right away from the vessel, a boat that was standing by,
They had seen our forms on the vessel as the flames lit up the sky.

I shouted a prayer to Heaven, they called for my wife, and she
Tore with new strength at my fetters—God helped her and I was free;
Then over the burning bulwarks we leaped for one chance of life.
Did they save us? Well, here I am, sir, and yonder's my dear old wife.

We were out in the boat till daylight, when a great ship passing by
Took us on board and at Melbourne landed us by and by.
We've played many parts in dramas since we went on that famous trip,
But ne'er such a scene together as we had on the burning ship!

THE PRIZE FIGHT

Index of Song Titles

Abdullah Bul-Bul Amir	*3*
Ach, Du Lieber Augustine	*17*
Actor's Story, The	*222*
Australian Highwayman's Song	*122*
Back and Side Go Bare, Go Bare!	*43*
Ballad of a Young Man	*174*
Ballad of Captain Kidd, The	*27*
Ballad of Lydia Pinkham, The	*46*
Band Played On, The	*6*
Bible Stories	*184*
Boston Burglar, The	*162*
Brother Noah	*10*
Butcher's Boy, The	*12*
Caissons Are Rolling Along, The	*179*
Cannibal Maiden, The	*146*
Casey Jones	*13*
Casey Jones II	*15*
Catch, A	*26*
Charming Young Widow I Met on the Train, The	*140*
Christofo Columbo	*18*
Clementine	*23*
Cocaine Bill and Morphine Sue	*150*
Cocaine Lil and Morphine Sue	*153*
Cowboy's Lament, The	*80*
Dis Mornin', Dis Evenin', So Soon	*200*
Dog-Catcher's Child, The	*176*
Don't Go in them Lions' Cage Tonight, Mother	*100*
Down Among the Dead Men	*55*
Down in Dear Old Greenwich Village	*128*
Drunkard John	*170*
Duckfoot Sue	*155*
Dying Fisherman's Song, The	*37*

Index of Song Titles

Dying Hobo, The	30
Dying Ranger, The	202
Face on the Bar-room Floor, The	82
Fair Fanny Moore	164
False Henry	139
Female Smuggler, The	132
Fill the Flowing Bowl	45
Flying Cloud, The	210
Foggy, Foggy Dew, The	26
Forty-nine Bottles	17
Get Away, Old Man, Get Away!	199
Girl in the Blue Velvet Band, The	213
Hail, Hail!	36
Hannah	145
Heenan and Sayers	136
Hell-bound Train, The	168
High Barbaree, The	102
Hop Head	143
Hop Song	157
I Had But Fifty Cents	38
I Know Where They Are	41
I Wanta Go Home	17
I Wish I Was Single Again	71
I'll Give My Love a Cherry	194
I'm Full	41
In Bohemia Hall	220
In the Sweet Bye and Bye	17
It's the Sime the 'Ole World Over	56
It's the Sime the 'Ole World Over II	58
I've Been Workin' on the Railroad	39
I've Only Been Down to the Club	165
Je Donnerais Versailles	177
Jesse James	42
Jim Fisk, Jr.	195
Johnny Sands	158

Just a Wee Doch-an Dorris	36
Kid's Fight, The	96
Lamentable History of Frankie and Johnnie, The	31
Lasca	86
Le Chef de Gare	46
Letter Edged in Black, The	192
Life Is But a Game of Cards	147
Little Brown Jug	40
Little More Cider, A	160
Lucky Jim	161
Mademoiselle from Armentieres	78
Maid of Amsterdam	76
Marines' Song, The	105
Midnight Express, The	182
Millman Tragedy, The	217
Morning After, The	50
My Cottage by the Sea	167
Navy Fragment	16
O, Give Me a Home Where the Buffalo Roam	134
O! Susanna	8
Oh, No, John!	154
Oh! Oh! Oh! It's a Lovely War!	74
Old Grey Mare, The	29
Old Joe Clark	149
Once I Loved a Railroad Brakeman	173
One More Drink for the Four of Us	25
Oregon Trail, The	51
O'Slattery's Light Dragoons	52
'Ostler Joe	90
Our Gude-Man	124
Pack of Cards, A	117
Pictures from Life's Other Side	148
Railroad Bill	48

Recruit, The — 208
Rio Grande — 138
Rollicking Bill the Sailor — 151
Rolling Home — 72
Roving Gambler, The — 120

Sailor's Return, The — 178
Sally Brown — 207
Salvation Army Song — 144
Sam Bass — 9
Samuel Hall — 54
Seven Long Years — 190
Shanahan's Ould Shebeen — 205
Son of a Gambolier, The — 59
Springfield Mountain — 166
Sweet Rosie — 25

Texas Rangers — 152
That Tattooed French Lady — 59
There Is a Tavern in the Town — 62
Twenty Years Ago — 84

Wal, I Swan — 64
Water Boy — 61
Way Down Yonder in the Cornfield — 31
What's the Use? — 198
When I Die — 24
When You and I Were Young, Maggie — 188
Whiskey for My Johnny — 70
Willie the Weeper — 156
Wreck of the Old 97, The — 131

Young Charlotte — 66
Young Monroe at Gerry's Rock — 180

Index of First Lines and Choruses

A cannibal maid and her Hottentot blade	146
Ach du lieber Augustine, Augustine, Augustine	17
Adieu, adieu, kind friends, adieu, adieu, adieu	62
A gilded mirror, a polished bar	50
Ah! ha! My little lady, honey take a (sniff) off me	150
A hoss and a flea an' a little mice	26
A lady once she had a lovely daughter	100
A little more cider, and a little more cider, too	160
And now we are aged and gray, Maggie	188
A-roving, a-roving, since a-roving's been my ruin	76
As I walked out in the streets of Laredo	80
A Texas cowboy on a bar-room floor had drunk so much he could hold no more	168
'Ave you heard of Sally Carter	58
Back and side go bare, go bare	43
Beside a western water tank, one cold November day	30
Both old and young, come ponder well, what I shall now relate	217
Brother Noah, Brother Noah, may I come into the Ark of the Lord	10
Call all hands to man the capstan	72
Casey would waltz with a strawberry blonde	6
Charlotte lived by the mountainside	66
Cocaine Bill and Morphine Sue, strolling down the avenue	150
Come all ye true-born shanty boys, wherever you may be	180
Come all you rounders for I want you to hear	15
Come all you rounders if you want to hear	13
Come, all you Texas rangers, wherever you may be	152
Come, landlord, fill the flowing bowl	45
Did you ever hear about Cocaine Lil	153
Did you ever hear tell about Willie the weeper	156
Down in yonder cottage, all forsaken and forlorn	164
For I am a weaver and I live all alone	26

For now I'll sing to you of the girl I love so true	155
Forty-nine bottles hanging on the wall	17
Frankie and Johnnie were lovers	31
From the Halls of Montezuma to the shores of Tripoli	105
Ha, ha, ha, 'tis you and me	40
Hail, hail, the gang's all here	36
Here's a health to the king and a lasting peace	55
He that drinketh strong beer and goes to bed right mellow	45
Home came the sailor, home from the sea	178
Hop Head went for a dreamy stroll	143
How the people held their breath	42
I am a roving gambler, I've gambled all around	120
I came from Alabama wid my banjo on my knee	8
I don't like Old Joe Clark	149
If you listen awhile, I'll sing you a song	195
If you want to find the Majors	41
I live in Vermont, and one morning last summer	140
I'll give my love a cherry without a stone	194
I'm a rambling rake of poverty	59
I'm full, absolutely full	41
In a cavern, in a canyon excavating for a mine	23
In Amsterdam there dwelt a maid	76
In Bohemia Hall, in Bohemia Hall where every man is king	220
In fourteen hundred and ninety-two, down in a Spanish alley	18
In Jersey City, where I did dwell, a butcher's boy I loved so well	12
In my cottage by the seashore	167
In that city of wealth, beauty and fashion	213
I run the old mill over here in Reubensville	64
I stood at eve where the sun went down	90
I took my girl to a ball last night	38
It was on the sixteenth day of April that they agreed to fight	136
I've been workin' on the railroad	39
I've got a girl named Hannah	145
I wander'd to-day to the hill, Maggie	188
I wanta go home, I wanta go home	17
I want free life, and I want fresh air	86
I was born in Boston city, a town you all know well	162
I was drunk last night, drunk the night before	25

Index of First Lines and Choruses   *233*

I was standing by the window yesterday morning	*192*
Je donnerais Versailles pour avoir mon ami	*177*
"Jim Blake your wife is dying!"	*182*
Jim was my friend, till one unhappy day	*161*
Just a wee doch-an-dorris	*36*
Just a year ago tonight, mother, how sorrowful were we	*139*
Last night I was out rather late	*165*
Le chef de gare, il est coucou	*46*
Life is but a game of cards, which each one has to learn	*147*
Long haired preachers come out every night	*17*
Mademoiselle from Armentieres parlez-vous	*78*
Matt Casey formed a social club that beat the town for style	*6*
Mine is a wild, strange story, the strangest you ever heard	*222*
Miss Dinah when she goes to church she looks so neat and gay	*160*
My name is Edward Hallahan	*210*
My name is Samuel Hall, Samuel Hall	*54*
My name was William Kidd, when I sailed, when I sailed	*27*
My wife and I live all alone	*40*
Now, in sailor's clothing swell Jane did go	*132*
Now listen all you girls when you go to choose a man	*199*
O, give me a home where the buffalo roam	*134*
Oh G-L-O-R-Y, we are S-A-V-E-D	*144*
Oh, it's hi-hi-yee! for the field artillery	*179*
Oh, the captain went below	*16*
Oh the moon shines to-night on the river	*176*
Oh the sons of the prophet were valiant and brave	*3*
O I gi'e a shillin' to see that tattooed French lady	*59*
Old folks, young folks, everybody come	*184*
Once a jolly swag-man camped beside a billy bong	*122*
Once I loved a railroad brakeman	*173*
One night as I sat by my fireside so weary	*117*
On Springfield Mountain there did dwell	*166*
On yonder hill there stands a creature	*154*
O Sally Brown she's a bright mulatta	*207*
Our gude-man cam' home at e'en	*124*

Over hill and dale we have hit the dusty trail	179
O, whiskey is the life of man	70
Poor Jesse left a wife to mourn all her life	42
Railroad Bill, Railroad Bill, he never worked and he never will	48
Rich people now they don't take a drop	157
Rolling home, rolling home, rolling home across the sea	72
Sam Bass was born in Indiana, it was his native home	9
Seven long years I've been married	190
Sez Corporal Madden to Private McFadden	208
She was just a parson's daughter	56
Sing, oh sing of Lydia Pinkham	47
So go and leave me if you wish to; never let me cross your mind	173
Some call this the best old world that nature could contrive	198
Some folks say that a nigger won't steal	31
Sweet Rosie Levinsky	25
Tell old Bill, when he leaves home dis mornin'	200
The anchor is weighed and the sails they are set	138
The club had a meeting tonight, love	165
The earth was made in six days and finished on the seventh	184
The next scene was that of a gambler	148
The old grey mare ain't what she used to be	29
There is a tavern in the town, in the town	62
There was a man in our town, I think his name was Brown	144
There was a man named Johnny Sands who married Betty Hague	158
There was a young man, and he came to New York	174
There were two lofty ships from old England came	102
The sun was sinking in the west	202
They give him his orders at Monroe, Virginia	131
This is the tale that Cassidy told	205
'Twas a balmy summer evening and a goodly crowd was there	82
'Twas midnight on the ocean, not a street car was in sight	37
Twenty years ago today	84
Up to your waist in water, up to your eyes in slush	74
Us two was pals, the Kid and me	96

Wal, I swan, I must be getting on	64
Waltzing Matilda, waltzing Matilda	122
Water boy, where are you hidin'?	61
Way down South in Greenwich Village	128
Way down yander in the Wahee Mountains	51
When I die, don't bury me at all	24
When I was single, oh, then, oh, then	71
When we sing of Lydia Pinkham	46
"Who's that a-knocking at my door?"	151
You have heard of Julius Caesar and of great Napoleon, too	52
You might have lit a lamp upon the fiery nose of Drunkard John	170

A CATALOGUE OF SELECTED DOVER BOOKS
IN ALL FIELDS OF INTEREST

A CATALOGUE OF SELECTED DOVER BOOKS
IN ALL FIELDS OF INTEREST

AMERICA'S OLD MASTERS, James T. Flexner. Four men emerged unexpectedly from provincial 18th century America to leadership in European art: Benjamin West, J. S. Copley, C. R. Peale, Gilbert Stuart. Brilliant coverage of lives and contributions. Revised, 1967 edition. 69 plates. 365pp. of text.
21806-6 Paperbound $3.00

FIRST FLOWERS OF OUR WILDERNESS: AMERICAN PAINTING, THE COLONIAL PERIOD, James T. Flexner. Painters, and regional painting traditions from earliest Colonial times up to the emergence of Copley, West and Peale Sr., Foster, Gustavus Hesselius, Feke, John Smibert and many anonymous painters in the primitive manner. Engaging presentation, with 162 illustrations. xxii + 368pp.
22180-6 Paperbound $3.50

THE LIGHT OF DISTANT SKIES: AMERICAN PAINTING, 1760-1835, James T. Flexner. The great generation of early American painters goes to Europe to learn and to teach: West, Copley, Gilbert Stuart and others. Allston, Trumbull, Morse; also contemporary American painters—primitives, derivatives, academics—who remained in America. 102 illustrations. xiii + 306pp. 22179-2 Paperbound $3.50

A HISTORY OF THE RISE AND PROGRESS OF THE ARTS OF DESIGN IN THE UNITED STATES, William Dunlap. Much the richest mine of information on early American painters, sculptors, architects, engravers, miniaturists, etc. The only source of information for scores of artists, the major primary source for many others. Unabridged reprint of rare original 1834 edition, with new introduction by James T. Flexner, and 394 new illustrations. Edited by Rita Weiss. 6⅝ x 9⅝.
21695-0, 21696-9, 21697-7 Three volumes, Paperbound $15.00

EPOCHS OF CHINESE AND JAPANESE ART, Ernest F. Fenollosa. From primitive Chinese art to the 20th century, thorough history, explanation of every important art period and form, including Japanese woodcuts; main stress on China and Japan, but Tibet, Korea also included. Still unexcelled for its detailed, rich coverage of cultural background, aesthetic elements, diffusion studies, particularly of the historical period. 2nd, 1913 edition. 242 illustrations. lii + 439pp. of text.
20364-6, 20365-4 Two volumes, Paperbound $6.00

THE GENTLE ART OF MAKING ENEMIES, James A. M. Whistler. Greatest wit of his day deflates Oscar Wilde, Ruskin, Swinburne; strikes back at inane critics, exhibitions, art journalism; aesthetics of impressionist revolution in most striking form. Highly readable classic by great painter. Reproduction of edition designed by Whistler. Introduction by Alfred Werner. xxxvi + 334pp.
21875-9 Paperbound $3.00

CATALOGUE OF DOVER BOOKS

VISUAL ILLUSIONS: THEIR CAUSES, CHARACTERISTICS, AND APPLICATIONS, Matthew Luckiesh. Thorough description and discussion of optical illusion, geometric and perspective, particularly; size and shape distortions, illusions of color, of motion; natural illusions; use of illusion in art and magic, industry, etc. Most useful today with op art, also for classical art. Scores of effects illustrated. Introduction by William H. Ittleson. 100 illustrations. xxi + 252pp.
21530-X Paperbound $2.00

A HANDBOOK OF ANATOMY FOR ART STUDENTS, Arthur Thomson. Thorough, virtually exhaustive coverage of skeletal structure, musculature, etc. Full text, supplemented by anatomical diagrams and drawings and by photographs of undraped figures. Unique in its comparison of male and female forms, pointing out differences of contour, texture, form. 211 figures, 40 drawings, 86 photographs. xx + 459pp. 5⅜ x 8⅜.
21163-0 Paperbound $3.50

150 MASTERPIECES OF DRAWING, Selected by Anthony Toney. Full page reproductions of drawings from the early 16th to the end of the 18th century, all beautifully reproduced: Rembrandt, Michelangelo, Dürer, Fragonard, Urs, Graf, Wouwerman, many others. First-rate browsing book, model book for artists. xviii + 150pp. 8⅜ x 11¼.
21032-4 Paperbound $2.50

THE LATER WORK OF AUBREY BEARDSLEY, Aubrey Beardsley. Exotic, erotic, ironic masterpieces in full maturity: Comedy Ballet, Venus and Tannhauser, Pierrot, Lysistrata, Rape of the Lock, Savoy material, Ali Baba, Volpone, etc. This material revolutionized the art world, and is still powerful, fresh, brilliant. With *The Early Work*, all Beardsley's finest work. 174 plates, 2 in color. xiv + 176pp. 8⅛ x 11.
21817-1 Paperbound $3.00

DRAWINGS OF REMBRANDT, Rembrandt van Rijn. Complete reproduction of fabulously rare edition by Lippmann and Hofstede de Groot, completely reedited, updated, improved by Prof. Seymour Slive, Fogg Museum. Portraits, Biblical sketches, landscapes, Oriental types, nudes, episodes from classical mythology—All Rembrandt's fertile genius. Also selection of drawings by his pupils and followers. "Stunning volumes," *Saturday Review.* 550 illustrations. lxxviii + 552pp. 9⅛ x 12¼.
21485-0, 21486-9 Two volumes, Paperbound $10.00

THE DISASTERS OF WAR, Francisco Goya. One of the masterpieces of Western civilization—83 etchings that record Goya's shattering, bitter reaction to the Napoleonic war that swept through Spain after the insurrection of 1808 and to war in general. Reprint of the first edition, with three additional plates from Boston's Museum of Fine Arts. All plates facsimile size. Introduction by Philip Hofer, Fogg Museum. v + 97pp. 9⅜ x 8¼.
21872-4 Paperbound $2.00

GRAPHIC WORKS OF ODILON REDON. Largest collection of Redon's graphic works ever assembled: 172 lithographs, 28 etchings and engravings, 9 drawings. These include some of his most famous works. All the plates from *Odilon Redon: oeuvre graphique complet*, plus additional plates. New introduction and caption translations by Alfred Werner. 209 illustrations. xxvii + 209pp. 9⅛ x 12¼.
21966-8 Paperbound $4.50

CATALOGUE OF DOVER BOOKS

DESIGN BY ACCIDENT; A BOOK OF "ACCIDENTAL EFFECTS" FOR ARTISTS AND DESIGNERS, James F. O'Brien. Create your own unique, striking, imaginative effects by "controlled accident" interaction of materials: paints and lacquers, oil and water based paints, splatter, crackling materials, shatter, similar items. Everything you do will be different; first book on this limitless art, so useful to both fine artist and commercial artist. Full instructions. 192 plates showing "accidents," 8 in color. viii + 215pp. $8\frac{3}{8}$ x $11\frac{1}{4}$. 21942-9 Paperbound $3.75

THE BOOK OF SIGNS, Rudolf Koch. Famed German type designer draws 493 beautiful symbols: religious, mystical, alchemical, imperial, property marks, runes, etc. Remarkable fusion of traditional and modern. Good for suggestions of timelessness, smartness, modernity. Text. vi + 104pp. $6\frac{1}{8}$ x $9\frac{1}{4}$. 20162-7 Paperbound $1.25

HISTORY OF INDIAN AND INDONESIAN ART, Ananda K. Coomaraswamy. An unabridged republication of one of the finest books by a great scholar in Eastern art. Rich in descriptive material, history, social backgrounds; Sunga reliefs, Rajput paintings, Gupta temples, Burmese frescoes, textiles, jewelry, sculpture, etc. 400 photos. viii + 423pp. $6\frac{3}{8}$ x $9\frac{3}{4}$. 21436-2 Paperbound $5.00

PRIMITIVE ART, Franz Boas. America's foremost anthropologist surveys textiles, ceramics, woodcarving, basketry, metalwork, etc.; patterns, technology, creation of symbols, style origins. All areas of world, but very full on Northwest Coast Indians. More than 350 illustrations of baskets, boxes, totem poles, weapons, etc. 378 pp. 20025-6 Paperbound $3.00

THE GENTLEMAN AND CABINET MAKER'S DIRECTOR, Thomas Chippendale. Full reprint (third edition, 1762) of most influential furniture book of all time, by master cabinetmaker. 200 plates, illustrating chairs, sofas, mirrors, tables, cabinets, plus 24 photographs of surviving pieces. Biographical introduction by N. Bienenstock. vi + 249pp. $9\frac{7}{8}$ x $12\frac{3}{4}$. 21601-2 Paperbound $4.00

AMERICAN ANTIQUE FURNITURE, Edgar G. Miller, Jr. The basic coverage of all American furniture before 1840. Individual chapters cover type of furniture—clocks, tables, sideboards, etc.—chronologically, with inexhaustible wealth of data. More than 2100 photographs, all identified, commented on. Essential to all early American collectors. Introduction by H. E. Keyes. vi + 1106pp. $7\frac{7}{8}$ x $10\frac{3}{4}$. 21599-7, 21600-4 Two volumes, Paperbound $11.00

PENNSYLVANIA DUTCH AMERICAN FOLK ART, Henry J. Kauffman. 279 photos, 28 drawings of tulipware, Fraktur script, painted tinware, toys, flowered furniture, quilts, samplers, hex signs, house interiors, etc. Full descriptive text. Excellent for tourist, rewarding for designer, collector. Map. 146pp. $7\frac{7}{8}$ x $10\frac{3}{4}$. 21205-X Paperbound $2.50

EARLY NEW ENGLAND GRAVESTONE RUBBINGS, Edmund V. Gillon, Jr. 43 photographs, 226 carefully reproduced rubbings show heavily symbolic, sometimes macabre early gravestones, up to early 19th century. Remarkable early American primitive art, occasionally strikingly beautiful; always powerful. Text. xxvi + 207pp. $8\frac{3}{8}$ x $11\frac{1}{4}$. 21380-3 Paperbound $3.50

CATALOGUE OF DOVER BOOKS

ALPHABETS AND ORNAMENTS, Ernst Lehner. Well-known pictorial source for decorative alphabets, script examples, cartouches, frames, decorative title pages, calligraphic initials, borders, similar material. 14th to 19th century, mostly European. Useful in almost any graphic arts designing, varied styles. 750 illustrations. 256pp. 7 x 10. 21905-4 Paperbound $4.00

PAINTING: A CREATIVE APPROACH, Norman Colquhoun. For the beginner simple guide provides an instructive approach to painting: major stumbling blocks for beginner; overcoming them, technical points; paints and pigments; oil painting; watercolor and other media and color. New section on "plastic" paints. Glossary. Formerly *Paint Your Own Pictures.* 221pp. 22000-1 Paperbound $1.75

THE ENJOYMENT AND USE OF COLOR, Walter Sargent. Explanation of the relations between colors themselves and between colors in nature and art, including hundreds of little-known facts about color values, intensities, effects of high and low illumination, complementary colors. Many practical hints for painters, references to great masters. 7 color plates, 29 illustrations. x + 274pp.
20944-X Paperbound $2.75

THE NOTEBOOKS OF LEONARDO DA VINCI, compiled and edited by Jean Paul Richter. 1566 extracts from original manuscripts reveal the full range of Leonardo's versatile genius: all his writings on painting, sculpture, architecture, anatomy, astronomy, geography, topography, physiology, mining, music, etc., in both Italian and English, with 186 plates of manuscript pages and more than 500 additional drawings. Includes studies for the Last Supper, the lost Sforza monument, and other works. Total of xlvii + 866pp. 7⅞ x 10¾.
22572-0, 22573-9 Two volumes, Paperbound $11.00

MONTGOMERY WARD CATALOGUE OF 1895. Tea gowns, yards of flannel and pillow-case lace, stereoscopes, books of gospel hymns, the New Improved Singer Sewing Machine, side saddles, milk skimmers, straight-edged razors, high-button shoes, spittoons, and on and on . . . listing some 25,000 items, practically all illustrated. Essential to the shoppers of the 1890's, it is our truest record of the spirit of the period. Unaltered reprint of Issue No. 57, Spring and Summer 1895. Introduction by Boris Emmet. Innumerable illustrations. xiii + 624pp. 8½ x 11⅝.
22377-9 Paperbound $6.95

THE CRYSTAL PALACE EXHIBITION ILLUSTRATED CATALOGUE (LONDON, 1851). One of the wonders of the modern world—the Crystal Palace Exhibition in which all the nations of the civilized world exhibited their achievements in the arts and sciences—presented in an equally important illustrated catalogue. More than 1700 items pictured with accompanying text—ceramics, textiles, cast-iron work, carpets, pianos, sleds, razors, wall-papers, billiard tables, beehives, silverware and hundreds of other artifacts—represent the focal point of Victorian culture in the Western World. Probably the largest collection of Victorian decorative art ever assembled—indispensable for antiquarians and designers. Unabridged republication of the Art-Journal Catalogue of the Great Exhibition of 1851, with all terminal essays. New introduction by John Gloag, F.S.A. xxxiv + 426pp. 9 x 12.
22503-8 Paperbound $5.00

CATALOGUE OF DOVER BOOKS

A HISTORY OF COSTUME, Carl Köhler. Definitive history, based on surviving pieces of clothing primarily, and paintings, statues, etc. secondarily. Highly readable text, supplemented by 594 illustrations of costumes of the ancient Mediterranean peoples, Greece and Rome, the Teutonic prehistoric period; costumes of the Middle Ages, Renaissance, Baroque, 18th and 19th centuries. Clear, measured patterns are provided for many clothing articles. Approach is practical throughout. Enlarged by Emma von Sichart. 464pp. 21030-8 Paperbound $3.50

ORIENTAL RUGS, ANTIQUE AND MODERN, Walter A. Hawley. A complete and authoritative treatise on the Oriental rug—where they are made, by whom and how, designs and symbols, characteristics in detail of the six major groups, how to distinguish them and how to buy them. Detailed technical data is provided on periods, weaves, warps, wefts, textures, sides, ends and knots, although no technical background is required for an understanding. 11 color plates, 80 halftones, 4 maps. vi + 320pp. $6\frac{1}{8}$ x $9\frac{1}{8}$. 22366-3 Paperbound $5.00

TEN BOOKS ON ARCHITECTURE, Vitruvius. By any standards the most important book on architecture ever written. Early Roman discussion of aesthetics of building, construction methods, orders, sites, and every other aspect of architecture has inspired, instructed architecture for about 2,000 years. Stands behind Palladio, Michelangelo, Bramante, Wren, countless others. Definitive Morris H. Morgan translation. 68 illustrations. xii + 331pp. 20645-9 Paperbound $3.00

THE FOUR BOOKS OF ARCHITECTURE, Andrea Palladio. Translated into every major Western European language in the two centuries following its publication in 1570, this has been one of the most influential books in the history of architecture. Complete reprint of the 1738 Isaac Ware edition. New introduction by Adolf Placzek, Columbia Univ. 216 plates. xxii + 110pp. of text. $9\frac{1}{2}$ x $12\frac{3}{4}$. 21308-0 Clothbound $12.50

STICKS AND STONES: A STUDY OF AMERICAN ARCHITECTURE AND CIVILIZATION, Lewis Mumford. One of the great classics of American cultural history. American architecture from the medieval-inspired earliest forms to the early 20th century; evolution of structure and style, and reciprocal influences on environment. 21 photographic illustrations. 238pp. 20202-X Paperbound $2.00

THE AMERICAN BUILDER'S COMPANION, Asher Benjamin. The most widely used early 19th century architectural style and source book, for colonial up into Greek Revival periods. Extensive development of geometry of carpentering, construction of sashes, frames, doors, stairs; plans and elevations of domestic and other buildings. Hundreds of thousands of houses were built according to this book, now invaluable to historians, architects, restorers, etc. 1827 edition. 59 plates. 114pp. $7\frac{7}{8}$ x $10\frac{3}{4}$. 22236-5 Paperbound $3.50

DUTCH HOUSES IN THE HUDSON VALLEY BEFORE 1776, Helen Wilkinson Reynolds. The standard survey of the Dutch colonial house and outbuildings, with constructional features, decoration, and local history associated with individual homesteads. Introduction by Franklin D. Roosevelt. Map. 150 illustrations. 469pp. $6\frac{5}{8}$ x $9\frac{1}{4}$. 21469-9 Paperbound $5.00

CATALOGUE OF DOVER BOOKS

THE ARCHITECTURE OF COUNTRY HOUSES, Andrew J. Downing. Together with Vaux's *Villas and Cottages* this is the basic book for Hudson River Gothic architecture of the middle Victorian period. Full, sound discussions of general aspects of housing, architecture, style, decoration, furnishing, together with scores of detailed house plans, illustrations of specific buildings, accompanied by full text. Perhaps the most influential single American architectural book. 1850 edition. Introduction by J. Stewart Johnson. 321 figures, 34 architectural designs. xvi + 560pp.
22003-6 Paperbound $4.00

LOST EXAMPLES OF COLONIAL ARCHITECTURE, John Mead Howells. Full-page photographs of buildings that have disappeared or been so altered as to be denatured, including many designed by major early American architects. 245 plates. xvii + 248pp. 7⅞ x 10¾.
21143-6 Paperbound $3.50

DOMESTIC ARCHITECTURE OF THE AMERICAN COLONIES AND OF THE EARLY REPUBLIC, Fiske Kimball. Foremost architect and restorer of Williamsburg and Monticello covers nearly 200 homes between 1620-1825. Architectural details, construction, style features, special fixtures, floor plans, etc. Generally considered finest work in its area. 219 illustrations of houses, doorways, windows, capital mantels. xx + 314pp. 7⅞ x 10¾.
21743-4 Paperbound $4.00

EARLY AMERICAN ROOMS: 1650-1858, edited by Russell Hawes Kettell. Tour of 12 rooms, each representative of a different era in American history and each furnished, decorated, designed and occupied in the style of the era. 72 plans and elevations, 8-page color section, etc., show fabrics, wall papers, arrangements, etc. Full descriptive text. xvii + 200pp. of text. 8⅜ x 11¼.
21633-0 Paperbound $5.00

THE FITZWILLIAM VIRGINAL BOOK, edited by J. Fuller Maitland and W. B. Squire. Full modern printing of famous early 17th-century ms. volume of 300 works by Morley, Byrd, Bull, Gibbons, etc. For piano or other modern keyboard instrument; easy to read format. xxxvi + 938pp. 8⅜ x 11.
21068-5, 21069-3 Two volumes, Paperbound $10.00

KEYBOARD MUSIC, Johann Sebastian Bach. Bach Gesellschaft edition. A rich selection of Bach's masterpieces for the harpsichord: the six English Suites, six French Suites, the six Partitas (Clavierübung part I), the Goldberg Variations (Clavierübung part IV), the fifteen Two-Part Inventions and the fifteen Three-Part Sinfonias. Clearly reproduced on large sheets with ample margins; eminently playable. vi + 312pp. 8⅛ x 11.
22360-4 Paperbound $5.00

THE MUSIC OF BACH: AN INTRODUCTION, Charles Sanford Terry. A fine, nontechnical introduction to Bach's music, both instrumental and vocal. Covers organ music, chamber music, passion music, other types. Analyzes themes, developments, innovations. x + 114pp.
21075-8 Paperbound $1.50

BEETHOVEN AND HIS NINE SYMPHONIES, Sir George Grove. Noted British musicologist provides best history, analysis, commentary on symphonies. Very thorough, rigorously accurate; necessary to both advanced student and amateur music lover. 436 musical passages. vii + 407 pp.
20334-4 Paperbound $2.75

JOHANN SEBASTIAN BACH, Philipp Spitta. One of the great classics of musicology, this definitive analysis of Bach's music (and life) has never been surpassed. Lucid, nontechnical analyses of hundreds of pieces (30 pages devoted to St. Matthew Passion, 26 to B Minor Mass). Also includes major analysis of 18th-century music. 450 musical examples. 40-page musical supplement. Total of xx + 1799pp.
(EUK) 22278-0, 22279-9 Two volumes, Clothbound $17.50

MOZART AND HIS PIANO CONCERTOS, Cuthbert Girdlestone. The only full-length study of an important area of Mozart's creativity. Provides detailed analyses of all 23 concertos, traces inspirational sources. 417 musical examples. Second edition. 509pp. 21271-8 Paperbound $3.50

THE PERFECT WAGNERITE: A COMMENTARY ON THE NIBLUNG'S RING, George Bernard Shaw. Brilliant and still relevant criticism in remarkable essays on Wagner's Ring cycle, Shaw's ideas on political and social ideology behind the plots, role of Leitmotifs, vocal requisites, etc. Prefaces. xxi + 136pp.
(USO) 21707-8 Paperbound $1.75

DON GIOVANNI, W. A. Mozart. Complete libretto, modern English translation; biographies of composer and librettist; accounts of early performances and critical reaction. Lavishly illustrated. All the material you need to understand and appreciate this great work. Dover Opera Guide and Libretto Series; translated and introduced by Ellen Bleiler. 92 illustrations. 209pp.
21134-7 Paperbound $2.00

BASIC ELECTRICITY, U. S. Bureau of Naval Personel. Originally a training course, best non-technical coverage of basic theory of electricity and its applications. Fundamental concepts, batteries, circuits, conductors and wiring techniques, AC and DC, inductance and capacitance, generators, motors, transformers, magnetic amplifiers, synchros, servomechanisms, etc. Also covers blue-prints, electrical diagrams, etc. Many questions, with answers. 349 illustrations. x + 448pp. 6½ x 9¼.
20973-3 Paperbound $3.50

REPRODUCTION OF SOUND, Edgar Villchur. Thorough coverage for laymen of high fidelity systems, reproducing systems in general, needles, amplifiers, preamps, loudspeakers, feedback, explaining physical background. "A rare talent for making technicalities vividly comprehensible," R. Darrell, *High Fidelity*. 69 figures. iv + 92pp. 21515-6 Paperbound $1.35

HEAR ME TALKIN' TO YA: THE STORY OF JAZZ AS TOLD BY THE MEN WHO MADE IT, Nat Shapiro and Nat Hentoff. Louis Armstrong, Fats Waller, Jo Jones, Clarence Williams, Billy Holiday, Duke Ellington, Jelly Roll Morton and dozens of other jazz greats tell how it was in Chicago's South Side, New Orleans, depression Harlem and the modern West Coast as jazz was born and grew. xvi + 429pp.
21726-4 Paperbound $3.00

FABLES OF AESOP, translated by Sir Roger L'Estrange. A reproduction of the very rare 1931 Paris edition; a selection of the most interesting fables, together with 50 imaginative drawings by Alexander Calder. v + 128pp. 6½x9¼.
21780-9 Paperbound $1.50

CATALOGUE OF DOVER BOOKS

AGAINST THE GRAIN (A REBOURS), Joris K. Huysmans. Filled with weird images, evidences of a bizarre imagination, exotic experiments with hallucinatory drugs, rich tastes and smells and the diversions of its sybarite hero Duc Jean des Esseintes, this classic novel pushed 19th-century literary decadence to its limits. Full unabridged edition. Do not confuse this with abridged editions generally sold. Introduction by Havelock Ellis. xlix + 206pp. 22190-3 Paperbound $2.50

VARIORUM SHAKESPEARE: HAMLET. Edited by Horace H. Furness; a landmark of American scholarship. Exhaustive footnotes and appendices treat all doubtful words and phrases, as well as suggested critical emendations throughout the play's history. First volume contains editor's own text, collated with all Quartos and Folios. Second volume contains full first Quarto, translations of Shakespeare's sources (Belleforest, and Saxo Grammaticus), Der Bestrafte Brudermord, and many essays on critical and historical points of interest by major authorities of past and present. Includes details of staging and costuming over the years. By far the best edition available for serious students of Shakespeare. Total of xx + 905pp.
21004-9, 21005-7, 2 volumes, Paperbound $7.00

A LIFE OF WILLIAM SHAKESPEARE, Sir Sidney Lee. This is the standard life of Shakespeare, summarizing everything known about Shakespeare and his plays. Incredibly rich in material, broad in coverage, clear and judicious, it has served thousands as the best introduction to Shakespeare. 1931 edition. 9 plates. xxix + 792pp. 21967-4 Paperbound $3.75

MASTERS OF THE DRAMA, John Gassner. Most comprehensive history of the drama in print, covering every tradition from Greeks to modern Europe and America, including India, Far East, etc. Covers more than 800 dramatists, 2000 plays, with biographical material, plot summaries, theatre history, criticism, etc. "Best of its kind in English," *New Republic.* 77 illustrations. xxii + 890pp.
20100-7 Clothbound $10.00

THE EVOLUTION OF THE ENGLISH LANGUAGE, George McKnight. The growth of English, from the 14th century to the present. Unusual, non-technical account presents basic information in very interesting form: sound shifts, change in grammar and syntax, vocabulary growth, similar topics. Abundantly illustrated with quotations. Formerly *Modern English in the Making.* xii + 590pp.
21932-1 Paperbound $3.50

AN ETYMOLOGICAL DICTIONARY OF MODERN ENGLISH, Ernest Weekley. Fullest, richest work of its sort, by foremost British lexicographer. Detailed word histories, including many colloquial and archaic words; extensive quotations. Do not confuse this with the Concise Etymological Dictionary, which is much abridged. Total of xxvii + 830pp. 6½ x 9¼.
21873-2, 21874-0 Two volumes, Paperbound $7.90

FLATLAND: A ROMANCE OF MANY DIMENSIONS, E. A. Abbott. Classic of science-fiction explores ramifications of life in a two-dimensional world, and what happens when a three-dimensional being intrudes. Amusing reading, but also useful as introduction to thought about hyperspace. Introduction by Banesh Hoffmann. 16 illustrations. xx + 103pp. 20001-9 Paperbound $1.00

CATALOGUE OF DOVER BOOKS

POEMS OF ANNE BRADSTREET, edited with an introduction by Robert Hutchinson. A new selection of poems by America's first poet and perhaps the first significant woman poet in the English language. 48 poems display her development in works of considerable variety—love poems, domestic poems, religious meditations, formal elegies, "quaternions," etc. Notes, bibliography. viii + 222pp.
22160-1 Paperbound $2.50

THREE GOTHIC NOVELS: THE CASTLE OF OTRANTO BY HORACE WALPOLE; VATHEK BY WILLIAM BECKFORD; THE VAMPYRE BY JOHN POLIDORI, WITH FRAGMENT OF A NOVEL BY LORD BYRON, edited by E. F. Bleiler. The first Gothic novel, by Walpole; the finest Oriental tale in English, by Beckford; powerful Romantic supernatural story in versions by Polidori and Byron. All extremely important in history of literature; all still exciting, packed with supernatural thrills, ghosts, haunted castles, magic, etc. xl + 291pp.
21232-7 Paperbound $2.50

THE BEST TALES OF HOFFMANN, E. T. A. Hoffmann. 10 of Hoffmann's most important stories, in modern re-editions of standard translations: Nutcracker and the King of Mice, Signor Formica, Automata, The Sandman, Rath Krespel, The Golden Flowerpot, Master Martin the Cooper, The Mines of Falun, The King's Betrothed, A New Year's Eve Adventure. 7 illustrations by Hoffmann. Edited by E. F. Bleiler. xxxix + 419pp.
21793-0 Paperbound $3.00

GHOST AND HORROR STORIES OF AMBROSE BIERCE, Ambrose Bierce. 23 strikingly modern stories of the horrors latent in the human mind: The Eyes of the Panther, The Damned Thing, An Occurrence at Owl Creek Bridge, An Inhabitant of Carcosa, etc., plus the dream-essay, Visions of the Night. Edited by E. F. Bleiler. xxii + 199pp.
20767-6 Paperbound $1.50

BEST GHOST STORIES OF J. S. LEFANU, J. Sheridan LeFanu. Finest stories by Victorian master often considered greatest supernatural writer of all. Carmilla, Green Tea, The Haunted Baronet, The Familiar, and 12 others. Most never before available in the U. S. A. Edited by E. F. Bleiler. 8 illustrations from Victorian publications. xvii + 467pp.
20415-4 Paperbound $3.00

MATHEMATICAL FOUNDATIONS OF INFORMATION THEORY, A. I. Khinchin. Comprehensive introduction to work of Shannon, McMillan, Feinstein and Khinchin, placing these investigations on a rigorous mathematical basis. Covers entropy concept in probability theory, uniqueness theorem, Shannon's inequality, ergodic sources, the E property, martingale concept, noise, Feinstein's fundamental lemma, Shanon's first and second theorems. Translated by R. A. Silverman and M. D. Friedman. iii + 120pp.
60434-9 Paperbound $2.00

SEVEN SCIENCE FICTION NOVELS, H. G. Wells. The standard collection of the great novels. Complete, unabridged. *First Men in the Moon, Island of Dr. Moreau, War of the Worlds, Food of the Gods, Invisible Man, Time Machine, In the Days of the Comet.* Not only science fiction fans, but every educated person owes it to himself to read these novels. 1015pp. (USO) 20264-X Clothbound $6.00

CATALOGUE OF DOVER BOOKS

LAST AND FIRST MEN AND STAR MAKER, TWO SCIENCE FICTION NOVELS, Olaf Stapledon. Greatest future histories in science fiction. In the first, human intelligence is the "hero," through strange paths of evolution, interplanetary invasions, incredible technologies, near extinctions and reemergences. Star Maker describes the quest of a band of star rovers for intelligence itself, through time and space: weird inhuman civilizations, crustacean minds, symbiotic worlds, etc. Complete, unabridged. v + 438pp. (USO) 21962-3 Paperbound $2.50

THREE PROPHETIC NOVELS, H. G. WELLS. Stages of a consistently planned future for mankind. *When the Sleeper Wakes,* and *A Story of the Days to Come,* anticipate *Brave New World* and *1984,* in the 21st Century; *The Time Machine,* only complete version in print, shows farther future and the end of mankind. All show Wells's greatest gifts as storyteller and novelist. Edited by E. F. Bleiler. x + 335pp. (USO) 20605-X Paperbound $2.50

THE DEVIL'S DICTIONARY, Ambrose Bierce. America's own Oscar Wilde—Ambrose Bierce—offers his barbed iconoclastic wisdom in over 1,000 definitions hailed by H. L. Mencken as "some of the most gorgeous witticisms in the English language." 145pp. 20487-1 Paperbound $1.25

MAX AND MORITZ, Wilhelm Busch. Great children's classic, father of comic strip, of two bad boys, Max and Moritz. Also Ker and Plunk (Plisch und Plumm), Cat and Mouse, Deceitful Henry, Ice-Peter, The Boy and the Pipe, and five other pieces. Original German, with English translation. Edited by H. Arthur Klein; translations by various hands and H. Arthur Klein. vi + 216pp.
20181-3 Paperbound $2.00

PIGS IS PIGS AND OTHER FAVORITES, Ellis Parker Butler. The title story is one of the best humor short stories, as Mike Flannery obfuscates biology and English. Also included, That Pup of Murchison's, The Great American Pie Company, and Perkins of Portland. 14 illustrations. v + 109pp. 21532-6 Paperbound $1.25

THE PETERKIN PAPERS, Lucretia P. Hale. It takes genius to be as stupidly mad as the Peterkins, as they decide to become wise, celebrate the "Fourth," keep a cow, and otherwise strain the resources of the Lady from Philadelphia. Basic book of American humor. 153 illustrations. 219pp. 20794-3 Paperbound $2.00

PERRAULT'S FAIRY TALES, translated by A. E. Johnson and S. R. Littlewood, with 34 full-page illustrations by Gustave Doré. All the original Perrault stories—Cinderella, Sleeping Beauty, Bluebeard, Little Red Riding Hood, Puss in Boots, Tom Thumb, etc.—with their witty verse morals and the magnificent illustrations of Doré. One of the five or six great books of European fairy tales. viii + 117pp. 8⅛ x 11. 22311-6 Paperbound $2.00

OLD HUNGARIAN FAIRY TALES, Baroness Orczy. Favorites translated and adapted by author of the *Scarlet Pimpernel.* Eight fairy tales include "The Suitors of Princess Fire-Fly," "The Twin Hunchbacks," "Mr. Cuttlefish's Love Story," and "The Enchanted Cat." This little volume of magic and adventure will captivate children as it has for generations. 90 drawings by Montagu Barstow. 96pp.
(USO) 22293-4 Paperbound $1.95

CATALOGUE OF DOVER BOOKS

THE RED FAIRY BOOK, Andrew Lang. Lang's color fairy books have long been children's favorites. This volume includes Rapunzel, Jack and the Bean-stalk and 35 other stories, familiar and unfamiliar. 4 plates, 93 illustrations x + 367pp.
21673-X Paperbound $2.50

THE BLUE FAIRY BOOK, Andrew Lang. Lang's tales come from all countries and all times. Here are 37 tales from Grimm, the Arabian Nights, Greek Mythology, and other fascinating sources. 8 plates, 130 illustrations. xi + 390pp.
21437-0 Paperbound $2.50

HOUSEHOLD STORIES BY THE BROTHERS GRIMM. Classic English-language edition of the well-known tales — Rumpelstiltskin, Snow White, Hansel and Gretel, The Twelve Brothers, Faithful John, Rapunzel, Tom Thumb (52 stories in all). Translated into simple, straightforward English by Lucy Crane. Ornamented with headpieces, vignettes, elaborate decorative initials and a dozen full-page illustrations by Walter Crane. x + 269pp. 21080-4 Paperbound **$2.00**

THE MERRY ADVENTURES OF ROBIN HOOD, Howard Pyle. The finest modern versions of the traditional ballads and tales about the great English outlaw. Howard Pyle's complete prose version, with every word, every illustration of the first edition. Do not confuse this facsimile of the original (1883) with modern editions that change text or illustrations. 23 plates plus many page decorations. xxii + 296pp.
22043-5 Paperbound $2.50

THE STORY OF KING ARTHUR AND HIS KNIGHTS, Howard Pyle. The finest children's version of the life of King Arthur; brilliantly retold by Pyle, with 48 of his most imaginative illustrations. xviii + 313pp. 6⅛ x 9¼.
21445-1 Paperbound $2.50

THE WONDERFUL WIZARD OF OZ, L. Frank Baum. America's finest children's book in facsimile of first edition with all Denslow illustrations in full color. The edition a child should have. Introduction by Martin Gardner. 23 color plates, scores of drawings. iv + 267pp. 20691-2 Paperbound $2.50

THE MARVELOUS LAND OF OZ, L. Frank Baum. The second Oz book, every bit as imaginative as the Wizard. The hero is a boy named Tip, but the Scarecrow and the Tin Woodman are back, as is the Oz magic. 16 color plates, 120 drawings by John R. Neill. 287pp. 20692-0 Paperbound $2.50

THE MAGICAL MONARCH OF MO, L. Frank Baum. Remarkable adventures in a land even stranger than Oz. The best of Baum's books not in the Oz series. 15 color plates and dozens of drawings by Frank Verbeck. xviii + 237pp.
21892-9 Paperbound $2.25

THE BAD CHILD'S BOOK OF BEASTS, MORE BEASTS FOR WORSE CHILDREN, A MORAL ALPHABET, Hilaire Belloc. Three complete humor classics in one volume. Be kind to the frog, and do not call him names . . . and 28 other whimsical animals. Familiar favorites and some not so well known. Illustrated by Basil Blackwell. 156pp. (USO) 20749-8 Paperbound $1.50

CATALOGUE OF DOVER BOOKS

EAST O' THE SUN AND WEST O' THE MOON, George W. Dasent. Considered the best of all translations of these Norwegian folk tales, this collection has been enjoyed by generations of children (and folklorists too). Includes True and Untrue, Why the Sea is Salt, East O' the Sun and West O' the Moon, Why the Bear is Stumpy-Tailed, Boots and the Troll, The Cock and the Hen, Rich Peter the Pedlar, and 52 more. The only edition with all 59 tales. 77 illustrations by Erik Werenskiold and Theodor Kittelsen. xv + 418pp. 22521-6 Paperbound $3.50

GOOPS AND HOW TO BE THEM, Gelett Burgess. Classic of tongue-in-cheek humor, masquerading as etiquette book. 87 verses, twice as many cartoons, show mischievous Goops as they demonstrate to children virtues of table manners, neatness, courtesy, etc. Favorite for generations. viii + 88pp. 6½ x 9¼.
22233-0 Paperbound $1.25

ALICE'S ADVENTURES UNDER GROUND, Lewis Carroll. The first version, quite different from the final *Alice in Wonderland,* printed out by Carroll himself with his own illustrations. Complete facsimile of the "million dollar" manuscript Carroll gave to Alice Liddell in 1864. Introduction by Martin Gardner. viii + 96pp. Title and dedication pages in color. 21482-6 Paperbound $1.25

THE BROWNIES, THEIR BOOK, Palmer Cox. Small as mice, cunning as foxes, exuberant and full of mischief, the Brownies go to the zoo, toy shop, seashore, circus, etc., in 24 verse adventures and 266 illustrations. Long a favorite, since their first appearance in St. Nicholas Magazine. xi + 144pp. 6⅝ x 9¼.
21265-3 Paperbound $1.75

SONGS OF CHILDHOOD, Walter De La Mare. Published (under the pseudonym Walter Ramal) when De La Mare was only 29, this charming collection has long been a favorite children's book. A facsimile of the first edition in paper, the 47 poems capture the simplicity of the nursery rhyme and the ballad, including such lyrics as I Met Eve, Tartary, The Silver Penny. vii + 106pp. (USO) 21972-0 Paperbound $1.25

THE COMPLETE NONSENSE OF EDWARD LEAR, Edward Lear. The finest 19th-century humorist-cartoonist in full: all nonsense limericks, zany alphabets, Owl and Pussycat, songs, nonsense botany, and more than 500 illustrations by Lear himself. Edited by Holbrook Jackson. xxix + 287pp. (USO) 20167-8 Paperbound $2.00

BILLY WHISKERS: THE AUTOBIOGRAPHY OF A GOAT, Frances Trego Montgomery. A favorite of children since the early 20th century, here are the escapades of that rambunctious, irresistible and mischievous goat—Billy Whiskers. Much in the spirit of *Peck's Bad Boy,* this is a book that children never tire of reading or hearing. All the original familiar illustrations by W. H. Fry are included: 6 color plates, 18 black and white drawings. 159pp. 22345-0 Paperbound $2.00

MOTHER GOOSE MELODIES. Faithful republication of the fabulously rare Munroe and Francis "copyright 1833" Boston edition—the most important Mother Goose collection, usually referred to as the "original." Familiar rhymes plus many rare ones, with wonderful old woodcut illustrations. Edited by E. F. Bleiler. 128pp. 4½ x 6⅜. 22577-1 Paperbound $1.00

CATALOGUE OF DOVER BOOKS

TWO LITTLE SAVAGES; BEING THE ADVENTURES OF TWO BOYS WHO LIVED AS INDIANS AND WHAT THEY LEARNED, Ernest Thompson Seton. Great classic of nature and boyhood provides a vast range of woodlore in most palatable form, a genuinely entertaining story. Two farm boys build a teepee in woods and live in it for a month, working out Indian solutions to living problems, star lore, birds and animals, plants, etc. 293 illustrations. vii + 286pp.
20985-7 Paperbound $2.50

PETER PIPER'S PRACTICAL PRINCIPLES OF PLAIN & PERFECT PRONUNCIATION. Alliterative jingles and tongue-twisters of surprising charm, that made their first appearance in America about 1830. Republished in full with the spirited woodcut illustrations from this earliest American edition. 32pp. 4½ x 6⅜.
22560-7 Paperbound $1.00

SCIENCE EXPERIMENTS AND AMUSEMENTS FOR CHILDREN, Charles Vivian. 73 easy experiments, requiring only materials found at home or easily available, such as candles, coins, steel wool, etc.; illustrate basic phenomena like vacuum, simple chemical reaction, etc. All safe. Modern, well-planned. Formerly *Science Games for Children*. 102 photos, numerous drawings. 96pp. 6⅛ x 9¼.
21856-2 Paperbound $1.25

AN INTRODUCTION TO CHESS MOVES AND TACTICS SIMPLY EXPLAINED, Leonard Barden. Informal intermediate introduction, quite strong in explaining reasons for moves. Covers basic material, tactics, important openings, traps, positional play in middle game, end game. Attempts to isolate patterns and recurrent configurations. Formerly *Chess*. 58 figures. 102pp. (USO) 21210-6 Paperbound $1.25

LASKER'S MANUAL OF CHESS, Dr. Emanuel Lasker. Lasker was not only one of the five great World Champions, he was also one of the ablest expositors, theorists, and analysts. In many ways, his Manual, permeated with his philosophy of battle, filled with keen insights, is one of the greatest works ever written on chess. Filled with analyzed games by the great players. A single-volume library that will profit almost any chess player, beginner or master. 308 diagrams. xli x 349pp.
20640-8 Paperbound $2.75

THE MASTER BOOK OF MATHEMATICAL RECREATIONS, Fred Schuh. In opinion of many the finest work ever prepared on mathematical puzzles, stunts, recreations; exhaustively thorough explanations of mathematics involved, analysis of effects, citation of puzzles and games. Mathematics involved is elementary. Translated by F. Göbel. 194 figures. xxiv + 430pp.
22134-2 Paperbound $3.50

MATHEMATICS, MAGIC AND MYSTERY, Martin Gardner. Puzzle editor for Scientific American explains mathematics behind various mystifying tricks: card tricks, stage "mind reading," coin and match tricks, counting out games, geometric dissections, etc. Probability sets, theory of numbers clearly explained. Also provides more than 400 tricks, guaranteed to work, that you can do. 135 illustrations. xii + 176pp.
20335-2 Paperbound $1.75

CATALOGUE OF DOVER BOOKS

MATHEMATICAL PUZZLES FOR BEGINNERS AND ENTHUSIASTS, Geoffrey Mott-Smith. 189 puzzles from easy to difficult—involving arithmetic, logic, algebra, properties of digits, probability, etc.—for enjoyment and mental stimulus. Explanation of mathematical principles behind the puzzles. 135 illustrations. viii + 248pp.
20198-8 Paperbound $1.75

PAPER FOLDING FOR BEGINNERS, William D. Murray and Francis J. Rigney. Easiest book on the market, clearest instructions on making interesting, beautiful origami. Sail boats, cups, roosters, frogs that move legs, bonbon boxes, standing birds, etc. 40 projects; more than 275 diagrams and photographs. 94pp.
20713-7 Paperbound $1.00

TRICKS AND GAMES ON THE POOL TABLE, Fred Herrmann. 79 tricks and games—some solitaires, some for two or more players, some competitive games—to entertain you between formal games. Mystifying shots and throws, unusual caroms, tricks involving such props as cork, coins, a hat, etc. Formerly *Fun on the Pool Table*. 77 figures. 95pp.
21814-7 Paperbound $1.25

HAND SHADOWS TO BE THROWN UPON THE WALL: A SERIES OF NOVEL AND AMUSING FIGURES FORMED BY THE HAND, Henry Bursill. Delightful picturebook from great-grandfather's day shows how to make 18 different hand shadows: a bird that flies, duck that quacks, dog that wags his tail, camel, goose, deer, boy, turtle, etc. Only book of its sort. vi + 33pp. 6½ x 9¼.   21779-5 Paperbound $1.00

WHITTLING AND WOODCARVING, E. J. Tangerman. 18th printing of best book on market. "If you can cut a potato you can carve" toys and puzzles, chains, chessmen, caricatures, masks, frames, woodcut blocks, surface patterns, much more. Information on tools, woods, techniques. Also goes into serious wood sculpture from Middle Ages to present, East and West. 464 photos, figures. x + 293pp.
20965-2 Paperbound $2.00

HISTORY OF PHILOSOPHY, Julián Marias. Possibly the clearest, most easily followed, best planned, most useful one-volume history of philosophy on the market; neither skimpy nor overfull. Full details on system of every major philosopher and dozens of less important thinkers from pre-Socratics up to Existentialism and later. Strong on many European figures usually omitted. Has gone through dozens of editions in Europe. 1966 edition, translated by Stanley Appelbaum and Clarence Strowbridge. xviii + 505pp.
21739-6 Paperbound $3.50

YOGA: A SCIENTIFIC EVALUATION, Kovoor T. Behanan. Scientific but non-technical study of physiological results of yoga exercises; done under auspices of Yale U. Relations to Indian thought, to psychoanalysis, etc. 16 photos. xxiii + 270pp.
20505-3 Paperbound $2.50

Prices subject to change without notice.
Available at your book dealer or write for free catalogue to Dept. GI, Dover Publications, Inc., 180 Varick St., N. Y., N. Y. 10014. Dover publishes more than 150 books each year on science, elementary and advanced mathematics, biology, music, art, literary history, social sciences and other areas.